THE WAY **FORWARD**

Compliments of...
wesleyan publishing house
P.O. Box 50434
Indianapolis, IN 46250-0434

Call: 800.493.7539 • Fax: 800.788.3535
E-mail: wph@wesleyan.org • Online: www.wesleyan.org/wph
Please send copies of any review or mention.

THE WAY **FORWARD**

DISCOVERING THE CLASSIC MESSAGE
OF HOLINESS

Edited by
Matt LeRoy and Jeremy Summers

wesleyan
publishing
house

Indianapolis, Indiana

Copyright © 2007 by Wesleyan Publishing House
Published by Wesleyan Publishing House
Indianapolis, Indiana 46250
Printed in the United States of America
ISBN: 978-0-89827-356-4

Library of Congress Cataloging-in-Publication Data

The way forward : discovering the classic message of holiness / edited
by Matthew LeRoy and Jeremy Summers.
    p. cm.
    ISBN 978-0-89827-356-4
    1. Holiness. 2. Christian biography. I. LeRoy, Matthew. II. Summers,
Jeremy.
    BT767.W39 2007
    234'.8—dc22
                                2007035346

To the memory of my grandfather, Rev. Daniel Edwin LeRoy.
Courageous lover of God and others. Preacher and liver of the message.
To the memory of Dr. Virgil Mitchell. "Holiness ablaze, encased in the meek."
And to my wife Sarah. I am humbled by your love and belief in me.
—Matt LeRoy

To my great-grandfather, Melvin Snyder, who proclaimed the message of holiness.
To my mentor, Keith Drury, who reinforces the relevant message of holiness.
To my wife, Andrea, who inspires me to live out holiness.
—Jeremy Summers

ACKNOWLEDGMENTS

We would like to thank Don Cady, Larry Wilson, and Mark Moore from Wesleyan Publishing House for entrusting this project to a couple of rookies. We are honored by your belief in this book, and in us. Thank you.

We are deeply grateful for the voices of wisdom that helped shape this book from the beginning. Bob Black, Keith Drury, Dan LeRoy, Ken Collins, Joe Dongell, JD Walt and Josh LeRoy were invaluable resources. Thank you for your ideas, insight and encouragement.

And to the Fellowship. Thanks to Ryan Forbes, Keith Jagger, Josh LeRoy, and Justin Simmons for helping us wrestle with mystery and walk in grace. You are a brotherhood and a blessing to us.

We also thank the Asbury Seminary Library staff, the Francis Asbury Society staff, Kent Steinke, and Jared Kidwell for your assistance in completing this project. And of course, we can't forget the fine folks at Waffle House and Solomon's Porch for providing a 'creative environment' where ideas are born and nurtured.

And a special thanks to the youth and young adult pastors of The Wesleyan Church, who creatively live and teach a fresh kind of holiness in the hardest places. You are the movement.

CONTENTS

Foreword   11

Introduction   13

1. Thomas à Kempis
    Mark Moore   15

2. Jeremy Taylor
    Andrea Summers   24

3. William Law
    Keith Drury   32

4. Nikolaus Ludwig von Zinzendorf
    Kevin Wright   40

5. John Wesley
    Anthony Graham   48

6. Charles Wesley
    J. D. Walt   58

7. John Fletcher
    Josh LeRoy   70

8. Richard Allen
    Christy Libscomb   78

9. William Wilberforce
    Jeremy Summers   86

10. Orange Scott and Luther Lee
    Bob Black   94

11. Phoebe Palmer
    Leonard Sweet   103

12. B. T. Roberts
    Jeff Eckhart   112

13. Catherine Booth
    Jo Anne Lyon   118

14. Hannah Whitall Smith
    Melvin Dieter   128

15. Thomas Cook
    Earle Wilson   138

16. Samuel Logan Brengle
    Joseph Dongell   147

17. E. Stanley Jones
    Matt LeRoy   157

18. Roy S. Nicholson
    David Medders   166

19. Dennis F. Kinlaw
    Steve DeNeff   173

20. Keith Drury
    David Drury   183

FOREWORD

Growing up as the son of a "holiness" preacher, I assumed in my formative years almost everything we believed came directly from the Bible or John Wesley. After all, wouldn't a church named "Wesleyan" turn to John and Charles Wesley as the source of its doctrines? And didn't John Wesley himself declare he was a "man of one book"—the Bible?

I have since learned that denominations in the Wesleyan tradition, particularly those who adhere to John Wesley's emphasis on heart holiness, draw from a much deeper and broader stream. In addition to the Scriptures, Wesley found inspiration for his teachings in the ancient church fathers as well as writers of deep piety in his own time. In the years following Wesley's death, his ideas were transported to American soil, where other religious movements such as revivalism, Pentecostalism, and fundamentalism all shaped, and in some cases altered, his understanding of the sanctified life.

This collection of writings by predecessors and followers of Wesley provides a wonderful exercise for both mind and heart. For the mind, here is a scholarly study of the ideas that shaped the Wesleys' understanding of an altogether Christian, wholly consecrated to God. Persons of deep devotion, such as Jeremy Taylor and William Law, inspired Wesley to pursue deeper relationships that would culminate in perfect love for God and others. His multivolume publication of *A Christian Library*, comprised of reprints and abridged selections from numerous Christian authors, demonstrates that Wesley was a man of many books—the primary source being the Scriptures.

Equally fascinating to the analytical mind is the outworking of Wesley's doctrine of entire sanctification in the fertile soil of American spirituality. Such diverse forces as rugged individualism, camp-meeting fervor, and church growth dynamics all interplay with the Wesleyan call to entire sanctification. Even in the emerging-church movements we can still find new perspectives on holiness; these are both faithful to the passion of the Wesleys, yet relevant to a postmodern world that questions some of the basic assumptions that underlie our most sacred doctrines.

As you read the following passages, don't forget your heart. You will benefit much from simply reading them devotionally, letting the Spirit of God speak to your inner being through these champions of the holiness message. Preface your reading with a prayer that you might discover the life of God in your own soul in ways that mirror the passion for God you see in these saints. Distill the wine of spirituality from these authors and consider how it might be preserved in the wineskins of a post-Christian age and a secular society.

The call for holy living is a timeless call. Jeremy Summers and Matt LeRoy, youthful scholars and present-day itinerants, call us to look forward by looking backward. Like Charles Wesley, they urge us to fulfill our calling to serve the present age through a word of encouragement from those who served well in times past. We will benefit much from heeding their challenge to "give heart and mind and soul and strength to serve the King of kings."

—DR. CLARENCE (BUD) BENCE

INTRODUCTION

"THE WAY FORWARD IS THE WAY BACK."

These are the words of our professor of historical theology and Wesley studies, Dr. Kenneth J. Collins. In our time under his teaching at Asbury Theological Seminary, he has often returned to this call. How does Christianity respond with relevance to the changing culture? How do we, as believers in Christ, carve a path into the uncertain times before us? His answer: "The way forward is the way back."

This book is an attempt to walk that road; to forge a way forward for the holiness movement by tracing the way back to its roots; to map out a future through memory of the past. By doing so, we will be able to form a solid theological foundation from which to step into the days ahead.

In these pages, we seek to introduce you again to the classic message of holiness, captured in the words of its great heralds. We have selected twenty crucial writings from the voices that have shaped the holiness movement throughout history. A current leader from within and around the Church introduces each selection and featured author. These short introductory essays provide insight into the life of each author, and the impact of his or her writing on the Church and the world.

The writings are arranged in chronological order, listed according to the time in which the authors lived. At the core of this book is the work of the Wesley brothers. As the founders of Methodism, John and Charles Wesley sparked a worldwide movement by way of their prolific writing of sermons and songs and tireless preaching of a truth that had set their souls on fire. We begin this book with the writings that profoundly influenced their ideas on holy living, and continue by tracing the journey of this message through the generations that followed. The project concludes with two modern voices of holiness, offering new expressions of the classic theology.

A humble monk. A burning heart. A former slave turned founding bishop. A politician and a poet. Abolitionists and activists. Preachers, professors, reformers, and revolutionaries. Through these set-apart voices we witness the journey of the holiness message through the ages, and its timeless promise of God's far-reaching grace and transforming love.

We believe the message of holiness has something to say to us, today, and to this world, now. It speaks in tones of hope and expectation, resounding with the promise of perfected love. It offers the assurance of restoration and reconciliation with the Father, by way of the Son and the Holy Spirit. And it challenges us to embrace humility, submitting ourselves to the unrivaled reign of God. Now, more than ever, the world needs to experience, and we need to remember this grace that enables holiness of heart and life.

THOMAS Á **KEMPIS**

CHAPTER 1

VANITY OF VANITIES
AND ALL IS VANITY,
EXCEPT TO LOVE GOD
AND SERVE HIM ALONE.

INTRODUCTION

If Thomas à Kempis's (1380–1471) tombstone were engraved today, it might read, "Devoted Monk and Bestselling Author of *The Imitation of Christ*"—a fact that would certainly make the humble monastic uneasy. He never set out to write the next big thing, and in fact, the earliest manuscripts cited an anonymous writer, leading to a smidge of controversy as to the authorship once the book became a popular source of devotion. Most scholars affirm Thomas à Kempis as the author and all affirm the lasting impact that this book has had on the body of Christ for over five hundred years. From Saint Ignatius of Loyola and John Wesley to Thomas Merton and Archbishop Desmond Tutu, inspired Christian leaders have treasured the depth and focus of this spiritual classic.

In *A Plain Account of Christian Perfection*, Wesley shed some light as to what he gleaned from Thomas à Kempis:

In the year 1726, I met with Kempis's *Christian's Pattern*. The nature and extent of inward religion, the religion of the heart, now appeared to me in a stronger light than ever it had done before. I saw, that giving even all my life to God (supposing it possible to do this, and go no farther) would profit me nothing, unless I gave my heart, yea, all my heart, to Him.

. . . I saw, that "simplicity of intention, and purity of affection," one design in all we speak or do, and one desire ruling all our tempers, are indeed "the wings of the soul," without which she can never ascend to the mount of God.

This entire consecration of the heart is clearly pervasive in Wesley's message of holiness and has always been the shining star of holiness theology.

The excerpts that have been selected from *The Imitation* will serve well as an opener for this book, as we endeavor to trace the holiness message throughout the ages. In true monastic fashion, Thomas à Kempis cuts through the vain pursuits that so easily tempt us away from dedicating our whole selves to God. Some of his spiritual guidance will seem as relevant as if it were written in the Starbucks across the street instead of a fifteenth-century monastery. And some of it will seem exactly as if it were written in a fifteenth-century monastery. If you choose to explore this great work beyond the selected excerpts, don't get hung up on the ascetic letter of the law, grab hold of the spirit of entire consecration.

Before you continue on with the selection, ponder this thought from C. S. Lewis on reading ancient books:

18

Every age has its own outlook. It is specially good at seeing certain truths and specially liable to make certain mistakes. We all,
therefore, need the books that will correct the characteristic
mistakes of our own period. And that means the old books.

. . . Not, of course, that there is any magic about the past.
People were no cleverer then than they are now; they made as
many mistakes as we. But not the same mistakes. They will not
flatter us in the errors we are already committing; and their own
errors, being now open and palpable, will not endanger us.

—MARK MOORE

THE IMITATION OF CHRIST

**THE FIRST CHAPTER: "IMITATING CHRIST AND DESPISING ALL VANITIES
ON EARTH"**

"He who follows Me, walks not in darkness," says the Lord. By
these words of Christ we are advised to imitate His life and habits, if
we wish to be truly enlightened and free from all blindness of heart.
Let our chief effort, therefore, be to study the life of Jesus Christ.

The teaching of Christ is more excellent than all the advice of the
saints, and he who has His spirit will find in it a hidden manna. Now,
there are many who hear the Gospel often but care little for it because
they have not the spirit of Christ. Yet whoever wishes to understand
fully the words of Christ must try to pattern his whole life on that of
Christ.

19

THOMAS Á KEMPIS

What good does it do to speak learnedly about the Trinity if, lacking humility, you displease the Trinity? Indeed it is not learning that makes a man holy and just, but a virtuous life makes him pleasing to God. I would rather feel contrition than know how to define it. For what would it profit us to know the whole Bible by heart and the principles of all the philosophers if we live without grace and the love of God? Vanity of vanities and all is vanity, except to love God and serve Him alone.

This is the greatest wisdom—to seek the kingdom of heaven through contempt of the world. It is vanity, therefore, to seek and trust in riches that perish. It is vanity also to court honor and to be puffed up with pride. It is vanity to follow the lusts of the body and to desire things for which severe punishment later must come. It is vanity to wish for long life and to care little about a well-spent life. It is vanity to be concerned with the present only and not to make provision for things to come. It is vanity to love what passes quickly and not to look ahead where eternal joy abides.

Often recall the proverb: "The eye is not satisfied with seeing nor the ear filled with hearing." Try, moreover, to turn your heart from the love of things visible and bring yourself to things invisible. For they who follow their own evil passions stain their consciences and lose the grace of God.

THE SEVENTH CHAPTER: "AVOIDING FALSE HOPE AND PRIDE"

Vain is the man who puts his trust in men, in created things.

Do not be ashamed to serve others for the love of Jesus Christ and to seem poor in this world. Do not be self-sufficient but place your trust in God. Do what lies in your power and God will aid your good will. Put no trust in your own learning nor in the cunning of any man, but rather in the grace of God Who helps the humble and humbles the proud.

If you have wealth, do not glory in it, nor in friends because they are powerful, but in God Who gives all things and Who desires above all to give Himself. Do not boast of personal stature or of physical beauty, qualities which are marred and destroyed by a little sickness. Do not take pride in your talent or ability, lest you displease God to Whom belongs all the natural gifts that you have.

Do not think yourself better than others lest, perhaps, you be accounted worse before God Who knows what is in man. Do not take pride in your good deeds, for God's judgments differ from those of men and what pleases them often displeases Him. If there is good in you, see more good in others, so that you may remain humble. It does no harm to esteem yourself less than anyone else, but it is very harmful to think yourself better than even one. The humble live in continuous peace, while in the hearts of the proud are envy and frequent anger.

THE THIRTEENTH CHAPTER: "RESISTING TEMPTATION"

So long as we live in this world we cannot escape suffering and temptation. Whence it is written in Job: "The life of man upon earth is a warfare." Everyone, therefore, must guard against temptation and must watch in prayer lest the devil, who never sleeps but goes about seeking whom he may devour, find occasion to deceive him. No one is so perfect or so holy but he is sometimes tempted; man cannot be altogether free from temptation.

Yet temptations, though troublesome and severe, are often useful to a man, for in them he is humbled, purified, and instructed. The

21

saints all passed through many temptations and trials to profit by them, while those who could not resist became reprobate and fell away. There is no state so holy, no place so secret that temptations and trials will not come. Man is never safe from them as long as he lives, for they come from within us—in sin we were born. When one temptation or trial passes, another comes; we shall always have something to suffer because we have lost the state of original blessedness.

Many people try to escape temptations, only to fall more deeply. We cannot conquer simply by fleeing, but by patience and true humility we become stronger than all our enemies. The man who only shuns temptations outwardly and does not uproot them will make little progress; indeed they will quickly return, more violent than before.

Little by little, in patience and long-suffering you will overcome them, by the help of God rather than by severity and your own rash ways. Often take counsel when tempted; and do not be harsh with others who are tempted, but console them as you yourself would wish to be consoled.

The beginning of all temptation lies in a wavering mind and little trust in God, for as a rudderless ship is driven hither and yon by waves, so a careless and irresolute man is tempted in many ways. Fire tempers iron and temptation steels the just. Often we do not know what we can stand, but temptation shows us what we are.

Above all, we must be especially alert against the beginnings of temptation, for the enemy is more easily conquered if he is refused admittance to the mind and is met beyond the threshold when he knocks.

Someone has said very aptly: "Resist the beginnings; remedies come too late, when by long delay the evil has gained strength." First, a mere thought comes to mind, then strong imagination, followed by pleasure, evil delight, and consent. Thus, because he is not resisted in the beginning, Satan gains full entry. And the longer a man delays in resisting, so much the weaker does he become each day, while the strength of the enemy grows against him.

Some suffer great temptations in the beginning of their conversion, others toward the end, while some are troubled almost constantly throughout their life. Others, again, are tempted but lightly according to the wisdom and justice of Divine Providence Who weighs the status and merit of each and prepares all for the salvation of His elect.

We should not despair, therefore, when we are tempted, but pray to God the more fervently that He may see fit to help us, for according to the word of Paul, He will make issue with temptation that we may be able to bear it. Let us humble our souls under the hand of God in every trial and temptation, for He will save and exalt the humble in spirit.

In temptations and trials the progress of a man is measured; in them opportunity for merit and virtue is made more manifest.

When a man is not troubled it is not hard for him to be fervent and devout, but if he bears up patiently in time of adversity, there is hope for great progress.

Some, guarded against great temptations, are frequently overcome by small ones in order that, humbled by their weakness in small trials, they may not presume on their own strength in great ones.

23

JEREMY **TAYLOR**

CHAPTER 2

HOLY INTENTION IS TO
THE ACTIONS OF A MAN
THAT WHICH THE SOUL
IS TO THE BODY.

INTRODUCTION

Jeremy Taylor (1613–1667) was a clergyman in the Church of England who lived some one hundred years before John Wesley. After completing studies at Cambridge, he was nominated by Archbishop Laud to a fellowship at All Souls College, Oxford. He then took on responsibility as chaplain-in-ordinary to King Charles I until he was imprisoned under Puritan rule. Eventually Taylor was forced into retirement as a family chaplain in Wales. After the Restoration of the Church of England, he was appointed Bishop of Down and Connor in Ireland and vice-chancellor of Trinity College in Dublin.

Taylor's poetic style of writing earned him the title "Shakespeare of the Divines." He wrote and preached with a mastery of metaphor and poetic imagination. His most well-known works, *The Rule and Exercises of Holy Living* and *The Rule and Exercises of Holy Dying*, provide a manual of Christian practice that has influenced devout readers for centuries.

Taylor wrote to correct the antinomianism of his day. Taylor and others like him contributed to a shift in seventeenth-century Anglicanism away from salvation by faith alone, to a more moralistic righteousness. His *Holy Living* put the responsibility of salvation on the individual, requiring some semblance of sanctification prior to salvation.

And so, this was the Anglican order of salvation John Wesley inherited. These works had a profound impression upon John Wesley. In developing the rules for the Holy Club at Oxford, Wesley borrowed heavily from Taylor's *Holy Living* in an effort to pursue a disciplined existence and do his best to live a godly life.

After Wesley picked up Taylor's book, he spent the next nine years fighting against sin and trying to fulfill the law of the gospel, believing that in holy living he would find salvation. But he did not, he wrote, have freedom from sin or the witness of the Spirit, because he searched for it not by faith, but by the works of the law. The Moravians eventually taught him something that Taylor did not: faith is intricately connected to salvation.

Wesley's Aldersgate experience in 1738 changed the way he viewed Taylor's work. Wesley emerged from Aldersgate with a commitment to salvation by faith only and a newfound assurance of salvation that emphasized God's immediate gift of faith and God's work to restore the image of God in the believer. Taylor's works had neglected the role of faith and assurance in salvation.

But Taylor's mark on Wesley's ministry was still unmistakable, because it was *Holy Living* and *Holy Dying* that pointed Wesley toward an important understanding of holiness, which he carried throughout 26 his life. Wesley learned from Taylor that sanctification is the process of being made actually holy, conformed to the image of God.

More specifically, Wesley attributed his own understanding of purity of intention to Taylor. Purity of intention, a hallmark of the Wesleyan understanding of holiness, was birthed for Wesley upon reading the following excerpt from Taylor's *Rules and Exercises for Holy Living*. Wesley acknowledged that an important truth he learned from Taylor was the significant role intentions played in action. It is purity of intention not just right action that determines holiness.

Jeremy Taylor was one of the most influential figures of the Church of England in the seventeenth century. But it was his gifted writing that allowed him to reach into future generations and influence the likes of John Wesley. Wesley's rejection of Taylor's order of salvation was not a rejection of all Taylor wrote and taught. Both Wesley and the holiness movement are indebted to Taylor and his understanding of what constitutes a biblical understanding of holiness.

—Andrea Summers

THE RULE AND EXERCISE
OF HOLY LIVING

THE SECOND GENERAL INSTRUMENT OF HOLY LIVING, PURITY OF INTENTION

That we should intend and design God's glory in every action we do, whether it be natural or chosen, is expressed by St. Paul, "Whether ye eat or drink, do all to the glory of God. Which rule, when we observe, every action of nature becomes religious, and every meal is

27

JEREMY TAYLOR

an act of worship, and shall have its reward in its proportion, as well as an act of prayer. Blessed be that grace and goodness of God, which, out of infinite desire to glorify and save mankind, would make the very works of nature capable of becoming acts of virtue, that all our life-time we may do Him service.

This grace is so excellent that it sanctifies the most common action of our life; and yet so necessary that, without it, the very best actions of our devotion are imperfect and vicious. For he that prays out of custom, or gives alms for praise, or fasts to be accounted religious, is but a pharisee hypocrite in his fast. But a holy end sanctifies all these and all other actions, which can be made holy, and gives distinction to them, and procures acceptance.

For, as to know the end distinguishes a man from a beast, so to choose a good end distinguishes him from an evil man. Hezekiah repeated his good deeds upon his sick-bed, and obtained favour of God, but the pharisee was accounted insolent for doing the same thing: because this man did it to upbraid his brother, the other to obtain a mercy of God. Zacharias questioned with the angel about his message, and was made speechless for his incredulity; but the blessed Virgin Mary questioned too, and was blameless; for she did it to inquire after the manner of the thing, but he did not believe the thing itself; he doubted of God's power, or the truth of the messenger; but she only of her own incapacity. This was it which distinguished the mourning of David from the exclamation of Saul; the confession of Pharaoh from that of Manasses; the tears of Peter from the repentance of Judas: "for the praise is not in the deed done, but in the manner of its doing." If a man visits his sick friend, and watches at his pillow for charity's sake, and because of his old affection, we approve it; but if he does it in hope of legacy, he is a vulture, and only watches for the carcass. The same things are honest and dishonest: "the manner of doing them, and the end of the design, makes the separation."

Holy intention is to the actions of a man that which the soul is to the body, or form to its matter, or the root to the tree, or the sun to the world, or the fountain to a river, or the base to a pillar: for, without these, the body is a dead trunk, the matter is sluggish, the tree is a block, the world is darkness, the river is quickly dry, the pillar rushes into flatness and a ruin; and the action is sinful, or unprofitable and vain. The poor farmer that gave a dish of cold water to Artaxerxes was rewarded with a golden goblet; and he that gives the same to a disciple in the name of a disciple, shall have a crown; but if he gives water in dispute, when the disciple needs wine or a cordial, his reward shall be to want that water to cool his tongue.

RULES FOR OUR INTENTIONS

1. In every action reflect upon the end; and in your undertaking it, consider why you do it, and why you propound to yourself for a reward, and to your actions as its end.

2. Begin every action in the name of the Father, of the Son, and of the Holy Ghost; the meaning of which is, (1) that we be careful that we do not the action without the permission or warrant of God; (2) that we design it to the glory of God, if not in the direct action, yet at least in its consequence; if not in the particular, yet at least in the whole order of things and accidents; (3) that it may be so blessed that what you intend for innocent and holy purposes, may not, by any chance, or abuse, or misunderstanding of men, be turned into evil, or made the occasion of sin.

JEREMY TAYLOR

3. Let every action of concernment be begun with prayer, that God would not only bless the action, but sanctify your purpose; and made an oblation of the action to God: holy and well intended actions being the best oblations and presents we can make to God; and, when God is entitled to them, He will the rather keep the fire upon the altar bright and shining.

4. In the prosecution of the action, renew and re-enkindle your purpose by short ejaculations to these purposes: "Not unto us, O Lord, not unto us, but unto Thy name, let all praise be given;" and consider: "Now I am working the work of God; I am His servant, I am in a happy employment, I am doing my master's business, I am not at my own dispose, I am using His talents, and all the gain must be His": for then be sure, as the glory is His, so the reward shall be thine. If thou bringest His goods home with increase, He will make thee ruler over cities.

5. Have a care, that, while the altar thus sends up a holy flame, thou dost not suffer the birds to come and carry away the sacrifice: that is, let not that which began well, and was intended for God's glory, decline and end in thy own praise, or temporal satisfaction, or a sin….

6. If any accidental event, which was not first intended by thee, can come to pass, let it not be taken into thy purposes, not at all be made use of; as if, by telling a true story, you can do an ill turn to your enemy, by no means do it; but, when the temptation is found out, turn all thy enmity upon that.

7. In every more solemn action of religion join together many good ends, that the consideration of them may entertain all your affections; and that, when any one ceases, the purity of your intention may be supported by another supply. He that fasts only to tame a rebellious body, when he is provided of a remedy either in grace or nature, may

be tempted to leave off his fasting. But be that in his fast intends the mortification of every unruly appetite, and accustoming himself to bear the yoke of the Lord, a contempt of the pleasures of meat and drink, humiliation of all wilder thoughts, obedience and humility, austerity and charity, and the convenience and assistance to devotion, and to do an act of repentance; whatever happens, will have reason enough to make him to continue his purpose, and to sanctify it...

8. If any temptation to spoil your purpose happens in a religious duty, do not presently omit the action, but rather strive to rectify your intention, and to mortify the temptation....

9. In all actions which are of long continuance, deliberation, and abode, let your holy and pious intention be actual; that is, that it be, by a special prayer or action, by a peculiar act of resignation or oblation, given to God; but in smaller actions a pious habitual intention; that is, that it be included within your general care that no action have an ill end; and that it be comprehended in your general prayers, whereby you offer yourself and all you do to God's glory.

10. Call not every temporal end a defiling of thy intention, but only, (1) when it contradicts any of the ends of God; or (2) when it is principally intended in an action of religion. For sometimes a temporal end is part of our duty; and such are all the actions of our calling, whether our employment be religious or civil....

But because many cases may happen in which a man's heart may deceive him, and he may not well know what is in his own spirit; therefore, by these following signs, we shall best make a judgment whether our intentions be pure and our purposes holy.

31

WILLIAM **LAW**

CHAPTER 3

INTRODUCTION

William Law (1686–1761), English minister and writer, was born seventeen years before John Wesley. He had first served in the Church of England but at age twenty-eight refused to take the oath of allegiance to George I and never served again in the state-sponsored church. Instead he became a tutor and advisor to the father of the eminent historian Edward Gibbon and wrote numerous books and shorter works. He wrote in an era of rationalism, where the head ruled. He responded with pointed writing, calling for an emphasis on the heart and practical Christian piety in daily living. Besides his personal conversations with Wesley, two books especially influenced the thinking of Wesley and the holiness movement. When John Wesley was twenty-three years old, Law's *Treatise on Christian Perfection* was published, and two years later *A Serious Call to a Devout and Holy Life* was published. Law was greatly influenced by the Christian mystics, while Wesley and the holiness movement tended to be more practical, though they held common ground on Christian piety. Holiness thinking was not invented by John Wesley but has been common throughout Christian history, including at the time of Wesley.

The selection here is taken from *A Serious Call*, which continues to be Law's best-selling work and which influenced not only Wesley but holiness churches into this century.

In this selection here we see William Law's powerful emphasis on *intention*. He calls for purity of intention among Christians, which will produce purity of action. We do what we intend to do. Wesley (and the holiness movement) would teach that knowing right was not our problem—most Christians know what they should do, it was full intention to do it. Such pure intention to obey Christ fully comes from God's bringing to our hearts a "perfect love." When God brought to us His perfect love, we would then be enabled to fully love God and thus obey Him likewise—we obey Him because we love Him. Law's writing continues to influence our thinking on intentions.

But we also see Law's call for holiness in the everyday life of a tradesperson. He reserves his sharpest words, however, for the wealthy, as did John Wesley and most of the American Holiness Movement (until we became rich ourselves). We also see his condemnation of worldly amusements and pleasure-seeking, not because they are sin, but because they do not contribute to piety. Law believed, as did Wesley and the early Holiness Movement, that whatever did not contribute to making us more like Christ was "superfluous," and a serious Christian would avoid those time-wasters. In short, William Law expected a serious Christian to be totally absorbed by the pursuit of holiness in order to become a "*fully* devoted follower of Christ."

—KEITH DRURY

A SERIOUS CALL TO
A DEVOUT AND HOLY LIFE

CHAPTER II: "AN INQUIRY INTO THE REASON WHY THE GENERALITY OF CHRISTIANS FALL SO FAR SHORT OF THE HOLINESS AND DEVOTION OF CHRISTIANITY"

It was this general intention that made the primitive Christians such eminent instances of piety, and made the goodly fellowship of the saints, and all the glorious army of martyrs and confessors. And if you will here stop and ask yourselves why you are not as pious as the primitive Christians were, your own heart will tell you that it is neither through ignorance nor inability, but purely because you never thoroughly intended it. You observe the same Sunday worship that they did; and you are strict in it, because it is your full intention to be so. And when you as fully intend to be like them in their ordinary common life, when you intend to please God in all your actions, you will find it as possible as to be strictly exact in the service of the Church. And when you have this intention to please God in all your actions, as the happiest and best thing in the world, you will find in you as great an aversion to everything that is vain and impertinent in common life, whether of business or pleasure, as you now have to anything that is profane. You will be as fearful of living in any foolish way, either of spending your time or your fortune, as you are now fearful of neglecting the public worship.

Now, who that wants this general sincere intention can be reckoned a Christian? And yet if it was among Christians, it would change the whole face of the world: true piety and exemplary holiness would be as common and visible as buying and selling or any trade in life.

35

Again, let a tradesman but have this intention, and it will make him a saint in his shop; his everyday business will be a course of wise and reasonable actions, made holy to God, by being done in obedience to His will and pleasure. He will buy and sell, and labour and travel, because by so doing he can do some good to himself and others. But then, as nothing can please God but what is wise and reasonable and holy, so he will neither buy nor sell, nor labour in any other manner, nor to any other end, but such as may be shown to be wise and reasonable and holy. He will therefore consider not what arts or methods or application will soonest make him richer and greater than his brethren, or remove him from a shop to a life of state and pleasure; but he will consider what arts, what methods, what application can make worldly business most acceptable to God, and make a life of trade a life of holiness, devotion, and piety. This will be the temper and spirit of every tradesman; he cannot stop short of these degrees of piety, whenever it is his intention to please God in all his actions, as the best and happiest thing in the world. And on the other hand, whoever is not of this spirit and temper in his trade and profession, and does not carry it on only so far as is best subservient to a wise and holy and heavenly life, it is certain that he has not this intention; and yet without it, who can be shown to be a follower of Jesus Christ?

Again, let the gentleman of birth and fortune but have this intention, and you will see how it will carry him from every appearance of evil to every instance of piety and goodness. He cannot live by chance, or as humour and fancy carry him, because he knows that nothing can please God but a wise and regular course of life. He cannot live in idleness and indulgence, in sports and gaming, in pleasures and intemperance, in vain expenses and high living, because these things cannot be turned into means of piety and holiness or made so many parts of a wise and religious life. As he thus removes from all appearance of evil, so he hastens and aspires after every instance of goodness. He does not ask what is allowable and pardonable, but what is commendable and praiseworthy. He does not ask whether God will forgive the folly of our lives, the madness of our pleasures, the vanity of our expenses, the richness of our equipage, and the careless consumption of our time; but he asks whether God is pleased with these things or whether these are the appointed ways of gaining His favour. He does not inquire whether it be pardonable to hoard up money, to adorn ourselves with diamonds and gild our chariots, whilst the widow and the orphan, the sick and the prisoner, want to be relieved; but he asks whether God has required these things at our hands, whether we shall be called to account at the last day for the neglect of them; because it is not his intent to live in such ways as, for aught we know, God may perhaps pardon; but to be diligent in such ways as we know that God will infallibly reward.

He will not therefore look at the lives of Christians to learn how he ought to spend his estate, but he will look into the Scriptures and make every doctrine, parable, precept, or instruction that relates to rich men a law to himself in the use of his estate.

He will have nothing to do with costly apparel, because the rich man in the Gospel was clothed with purple and fine linen. He denies himself the pleasures and indulgences which his estate could procure, because our blessed Saviour saith, "Woe unto you that are rich! For ye have received your consolation" (Luke 6:24). He will have but one rule for charity, and that will be to spend all that he can that way, because the Judge of quick and dead hath said that all that is so given, is given to Him. He will have no hospitable table for the rich and wealthy to come and feast with him in good eating and drinking; because our blessed Lord saith, "When thou makest a dinner, call not thy friends, nor thy brethren, neither thy kinsman, nor thy rich neighbours, lest they also bid thee again, and a recompense be made thee. But when thou makest a feast, call the poor, the maimed, the lame, the blind: and thou shalt be blessed: for they cannot recompense thee: for thou shalt be recompensed at the resurrection of the just" (Luke 14:12–14).

He will waste no money in gilded roofs or costly furniture: he will not be carried from pleasure to pleasure in expensive state and equipage, because an inspired Apostle hath said that "all that is in the world, the lust of the flesh, the lust of the eyes, and the pride of life, is not of the Father, but is of the world" (1 John 2:16) . . .

… I have chosen to explain this matter by appealing to this intention, because it makes the case so plain, and because every one that has a mind may see it in the clearest light, and feel it in the strongest manner, only by looking into his own heart. For it is as easy for every person to know whether he intends to please God in all his actions as for any servant to know whether this be his intention towards his master. Every one also can as easily tell how he lays out his money, and whether he considers how to please God in it, as he can tell where his estate is, and whether it be in money or land. So that there is no plea left for ignorance or frailty as to this matter; everybody is in the light, and everybody has power. And no one can fail, but he that is not so much a Christian, as to intend to please God in the use of his estate.

You see two persons: one is regular in public and private prayer, the other is not. Now the reason of this difference is not this, that one has strength and power to observe prayer and the other has not; but the reason is this, that one intends to please God in the duties of devotion, and the other has no intention about it. Now the case is the same in the right or wrong use of our time and money. You see one person throwing away his time in sleep and idleness, in visiting and diversions, and his money in the most vain and unreasonable expenses. You see another careful of every day, dividing his hours by rules of reason and religion, and spending all his money in works of charity: now the difference is not owing to this, that one has strength and power to do thus, and the other has not; but it is owing to this, that one intends to please God in the right use of all his time and all his money, and the other has no intention about it.

WILLIAM LAW

NIKOLAUS LUDWIG VON ZINZENDORF

CHAPTER 4

FAITH IS HIS DUTY
AND HOLINESS
HIS NATURE.

INTRODUCTION

Those who trace their spiritual lineage back through the classic message of holiness will undoubtedly find themselves deeply indebted to a man by the name of Count Nikolaus Ludwig von Zinzendorf (1700–1760). Born into European nobility on May 26, 1700, Zinzendorf was just six weeks old when his father passed away, leaving the infant to be raised chiefly by his maternal grandmother, the baroness of Gersdorf. It was under his grandmother's care that Zinzendorf came into contact with leaders of a movement called Pietism, which promulgated the importance of the heart alongside the intellect within the Christian faith.

While touring an art museum in 1719, the adolescent Zinzendorf beheld a painting called *Ecce Homo*, depicting the crucified Christ along with the caption "This have I done for you—now what will you do for me?" Deeply moved by the profundity of the words and sensing that Christ had spoken them directly to his heart,

Zinzendorf dedicated his life to following wholeheartedly after Jesus.

In 1722, Zinzendorf granted permission to a group of Moravians to settle on his vast estate. The Moravians were a religious group convinced that humans are saved by faith alone and that faith must manifest itself in good works. Their song of spirituality resonated deeply within Zinzendorf's heart. Eventually, Zinzendorf resigned the duties and privileges of an aristocrat and dedicated his time toward leading the Moravian community known as Herrnhut.

Zinzendorf held to a Pietist-influenced theology centering on a deep conviction that faith is something apprehended in the heart before it makes its way into the head. Thus, to be a Christian is to know in one's heart that Jesus Christ has atoned for all sin through his precious blood shed on the cross.

In these selected passages from an address given by the Count in 1740, we see Zinzendorf acknowledging the fallenness of humanity but also remaining highly optimistic of the redeeming power of Christ's blood to not only forgive sin but to also diminish the desire to sin. Furthermore, Christians inherit an unshakeable assurance of their salvation accompanied by a holiness-induced happiness. Holy living is the natural consequence of one who daily carries around in his or her heart the remembrance of Jesus' sacrificial death on the cross. This holiness is available to all those who depend on Christ and cast themselves completely upon his boundless mercy. Thus, these passages are instrumental in helping us see that for Zinzendorf, personal holiness is no more complex or complicated than Jesus Christ.

42 This theology of the heart radically influenced both John and Charles Wesley as they came into direct contact with Zinzendorf and

his followers. Zinzendorf's conviction that one may have assurance of Christ's victory over sin's guilt and dominion helped the Wesley brothers to find peace for their restless and wandering hearts. It is of great significance, then, that the same holiness and happiness preached and experienced by Zinzendorf and the Wesley brothers is still available to all who earnestly seek it today.

—KEVIN WRIGHT

SIXTEEN DISCOURSES ON THE REDEMPTION OF MAN BY THE DEATH OF CHRIST

One need not to be so anxious how to avoid sin and lead a godly life, as how to learn to know Jesus one's Savior; the rest will follow of course, after the Son has made us free, for He alone can deliver us from sin, He can relieve, when all human means fall too short.

We cannot deny that we still have sin (1 John 1:8) and that we shall carry it to the grave. Wherefore the body is dead because of sin (Rom. 8) and subject to putrefaction. Our very nature and the whole mass of man is infected with the poison of sinful matter, the best remedy against which is its fermentation in the grave, that thus our Savior may produce something better. But although we carry this body of death still about us, yet in the Children of God, sin is to be looked upon as a banished, crucified and condemned thing, or as a malefactor and

43

prisoner who dare not lift up his head and domineer again. The old Man has had his sentence passed upon him by Christ that he shall die upon the cross and be annihilated (Rom. 6).

For this purpose, the Son of God was manifested, that he might destroy the works of the devil (1 John 3:8). To dissolve and tear the system of sin to pieces, that in the Faithful lust cannot be conceived, nor Sin bringing forth death (James 1:15; Matt. 5:28). But that sin must be always kept under foot and in subjection, and so lost its dominion and power more and more, that it dare not stir, or always expect a new death.

The faithful Believer dare not so much as give ear to sin, much less to enter into any struggle with it, but since the solemn divorce between the Soul and her old Husband through the Body of Christ is ratified, that he must abandon her, the Soul must now cleave to her right and lawful Husband and bring forth fruit to everlasting Life, *she is never willing nor desires to sin any more.* This privilege is a great happiness for us.

But this is not antecedent to grace, much less extended beyond grace, but this grace must be present and one must have received remission of sins, as an ungodly person, then this privilege follows and takes place. Then every one acknowledges himself a sinner in his degree and humbleth himself for the grace bestowed upon him, which is great in all and merited for all.

We are sinners as well with all our best performances and with all our enormities. And without Christ no good resolution to avoid sin and live godly avails anything. Wherefore our main and most important business ought to be to obtain faith in Christ, but cast off all other things and forget them as a child, and Jesus must come to be our faith, our love and hope, the whole and sole object and end of our life, so that all our thoughts, words, and desires be full of him; then they are right and approved by God for His sake. And then we dare not tremble like the devils by our faith, but can be sincere and confident like children.

A man without Christ is a slave to his pride, lust, avarice and cannot resist, but is dragged by their chains from one danger into another. But he that is in Christ overcomes all that, and becomes a lord over all his passions; neither doth he dare to sin any more, and if he durst, he would not. A member of Christ looks upon holiness and righteousness of life as a great happiness and benefit. Faith is his duty and holiness his nature, and whereas other men dispute with sin, wrestle and fight against it, and yet perhaps are overcome, according to the pathetic description of St. Paul (Rom. 7). The members of Christ are assured, that since death, the wages of sin, is under their feet, *all is yours, whether life or death* (1 Cor. 3:22). Since they slipped their necks out of the collar of the law, that kept them in bondage before *(but the law is the power of sin)*; sin must with a word be trod down to the ground and dare not rise, till we please ourselves.

Christians are Priests of God, who daily walk in their holy apparel and lift up holy hands without wrath and doubting. They keep themselves unpolluted from all things and purify themselves in the Blood of Christ, because they bear the Lord's vessels. But the chief duty of their priesthood is to carry the death and the bloody sacrifice of their Redeemer continually within their heart and diligently to enter into the Sanctuary.

In short, our redemption consists properly in this: The ever living Son of God, who is as truly the Son of God as any Man's son is a man, has been pleased, because sinners could be redeemed by no other 45 means, in the Love of His Father, through the cooperation of the Holy

Ghost, yet out of His free choice to humble himself and to be born a man in the form of sinful flesh, like as other children are to grow up by degrees, to be educated by His parents and live in subjection to them, to live thirty years incognito, so that His name is hardly mentioned all that time, to appear at last publicly to teach for three years, to work many miracles and give innumerable proofs of His truth and glory, gaining but few souls, without seeing His disciples in that state and disposition He wished them in, to suffer a most vile, shameful, and cursed death, in the eyes of all the world, to hang upon the cross as a malefactor between two most notorious thieves, to be railed at, spit upon, scored and mocked at, and all this with no other view, and to no other end, but to redeem the whole race of men from sin, Satan, Death, and hell; to take away the curse from the whole Earth and to restore the eternal righteousness, which had been lost by Sin, to exalt mercy above judgment, to gain a victory, the like the world has never heard nor will hear of, and thus in one moment by the resignation of his Spirit into the hands of his Father and laying down his life, to execute the best thought and design of Divine Wisdom, and which the Will, Counsel, and Love of God has resolved upon from all eternity: he rose afterwards and shewed himself to a few souls, teaching and explaining to them the mystery of the Kingdom more accurately and fully, that so they might become His witnesses in all the World: After all these transactions He ascended above all heavens, where He as Man sits at the Right Hand of Power, as the Head of all His faithful Believers to reign over all the World, but in the Form and Figure of the cross, wherein He and His Believers are looked upon as nothing, or as if they were made for nothing else but sufferings, and for a spectacle of angels and men.

46

He who knows the Salvation, that Jesus has purchased us with His bloody death on the cross, who has abolished Death, and brought Life and Immortality to Light, that sin can have no more dominion over us, because we are no more under the Law, but under grace; he understands the Mystery, how to get rid of Sin in a most easy manner without any difficulty, complaint, and torment, so that it must give way, must fly and die; Satan who has it in his hands, and uses it to lead men according to his pleasure, at last dare attack us no more. We either keep ourselves that the wicked one dare not touch us, or resist the Devil, that at last he must fly from us.

And so this is to be obtained no other way, than by an entire dependence upon our Savior's heroic and victorious power: When we receive of our Redeemer all his righteousness and merit, and humbly confess and say to him, "My blessed Savior! I of myself can do nothing, I am a man weary and heavy laden, have mercy on me, I scarce can breathe under the weight of sin, I cannot overcome it, deliver me from this Body of Death, and set me free from my perdition: Apply the efficacy of thy blood and death in the Mother-like compassion of thy heart to my soul: Do thou say to mine enemies: be gone: cast my sins behind thee, and swallow up death in victory:" Then will our Savior soon take our case in hand and receive us, who has said: *He that comes to me, I will in no way cast out.* He knows very well, that we can do nothing without Him.

NIKOLAUS LUDWIG VON ZINZENDORF

JOHN WESLEY

CHAPTER 5

INTRODUCTION

John Wesley (1703–1791) was an Anglican minister, Christian theologian, and founder of the Methodist Movement. He was born in Epworth, England, the fifteenth of nineteen children, on June 17, 1703. The son of Samuel and Susanna Wesley, he was greatly influenced by the Anglican tradition of his minister father and the Puritan heritage of his mother.

He received a scholarship to study at Oxford in 1720, where he and his brother Charles met a group of friends with a shared passion for God. This group included a young George Whitefield, the famous preacher who would go on to lead America's Great Awakening. Their zeal for God earned them the nickname the "Holy Club."

In 1735 he traveled with Charles to Georgia as a missionary to the Indians. His literal interpretation of the Bible crafted his belief that all men are created equal. This philosophy placed him at odds with many of the colonists. He returned to England after three years and became a lifelong opponent to slavery.

Wesley met two Moravian missionaries prior to his return to England who talked to him about salvation by faith alone in Jesus Christ. Discovering an absence of personal relationship with Jesus Christ, he wrestled for some time under strong conviction. On May 24, 1738, he heard a reading from *Luther's Commentary on Romans* at a meeting on London's Aldersgate Street. The emphasis on salvation by faith resonated in his soul. He would later describe the moment in his journal, saying, "I felt my heart strangely warmed."

Transformed by his experience, Wesley began to promote the Methodist movement by organizing Bible study and fellowship groups in England, Scotland, Wales, and Ireland. From there, he launched out with this message to other parts of the world. He believed that Christianity was central to meaningful living and so unashamedly shared his conviction on Christian perfection.

Wesley was an inexhaustible preacher and writer. A selection from one of his most famous works, *A Plain Account of Christian Perfection*, is featured here. This selection is critical for the careful consideration of all believers today. In it, he defines Christian perfection as "loving God with all our heart, mind, soul, and strength . . . governed by pure love." Though we live in a time when the quest for happiness has replaced the quest for holiness, our Lord's mandate remains clear. Holiness of heart and life is the foundation for upright living, and lifestyle holiness is the standard every Christian is expected to embrace. The fruit of the Spirit will never be evident in its fullness unless we submit to this process. If communities are to be transformed, it will only happen through believers who are filled

50

with God's Holy Spirit and are walking in obedience to God's Word.

John Wesley has been wonderfully used to bring to the forefront the aspiration of God for his people. This desire is not new but carefully and systematically declared throughout the canon of Scripture. From Genesis to Revelation, we read that God's requirement for believers is holiness. All over the world, men and women are endeavoring to live lives that are pleasing to God because John Wesley was willing to make a stand in his generation, proclaiming unashamedly that believers can be transformed by grace and perfected in love.

—ANTHONY GRAHAM

A PLAIN ACCOUNT
OF CHRISTIAN PERFECTION

17. On Monday, June 25, 1744, our First Conference began; six Clergymen and all our Preachers being present. The next morning we seriously considered the doctrine of sanctification, or perfection. The questions asked concerning it, and the substance of the answers given, were as follows:

QUESTION. *What is it to be sanctified?*

ANSWER. To be renewed in the image of God, "in righteousness and true holiness."

51

Q. *What is implied in being a perfect Christian?*

A. The loving God with all our heart, and mind, and soul (Deut. 6:5).

Q. *Does this imply that all inward sin is taken away?*

A. Undoubtedly; or how can we be said to be saved from all our "uncleannesses" (Ezek. 36:29)?

Our Second Conference began August 1, 1745. The next morning we spoke of sanctification as follows :

QUESTION. *When does inward sanctification begin?*

ANSWER. In the moment a man is justified. (Yet sin remains in him, yea, the seed of all sin, till he is sanctified throughout.) From that time a believer gradually dies to sin and grows in grace.

Q. *Is this ordinarily given till a little before death?*

A. It is not, to those who expect it no sooner.

Q. *But may we expect it sooner?*

A. Why not? For, although we grant (1) That the generality of believers, whom we have hitherto known, were not so sanctified till near death; (2) That few of those to whom St. Paul wrote his Epistles were so at that time; nor, (3) He himself at the time of writing his former Epistles; yet all this does not prove, that we may not be so today.

Q. In what manner should we preach sanctification?

A. Scarce at all to those who are not pressing forward: To those who are, always by way of promise; always drawing, rather than driving.

19. At the Conference in the year 1759, perceiving some danger that a diversity of sentiments should insensibly steal in among us, we again largely considered this doctrine; and soon after I published *Thoughts on Christian Perfection...*

QUESTION. *What is Christian perfection?*

ANSWER. The loving God with all our heart, mind, soul, and strength. This implies that no wrong temper, none contrary to love, remains in the soul; and that all the thoughts, words, and actions, are governed by pure love.

Q. *Do you affirm that this perfection excludes all infirmities, ignorance, and mistake?*

A. I continually affirm quite the contrary, and always have done so.

Q. *But how can every thought, word, and work, be governed by pure love, and the man be subject at the same time to ignorance and mistake?*

A. I see no contradiction here: "A man may be filled with pure love and still be liable to mistake." Indeed I do not expect to be freed from actual mistakes till this mortal puts on immortality. I believe this to be a natural consequence of the soul's dwelling in flesh and blood. For we cannot now think at all, but by the mediation of those bodily organs which have suffered equally with the rest of our frame. And hence we cannot avoid sometimes thinking wrong till this corruptible shall have put on incorruption.

But we may carry this thought farther yet. A mistake in judgment may possibly occasion a mistake in practice. Yet, where every word and action springs from love, such a mistake is not properly a sin. However, it cannot bear the rigour of God's justice, but needs the atoning blood.

Q. *Is this death to sin and renewal in love gradual or instantaneous?*

A. A man may be dying for some time; yet he does not, properly speaking, die till the instant the soul is separated from the body; and

53

in that instant he lives the life of eternity. In like manner, he may be dying to sin for some time; yet he is not dead to sin till sin is separated from his soul; and in that instant he lives the full life of love. And as the change undergone, when the body dies, is of a different kind, and infinitely greater than any we had known before, yea, such as till then it is impossible to conceive; so the change wrought, when the soul dies to sin, is of a different kind, and infinitely greater than any before, and than any can conceive till he experiences it. Yet he stills grows in grace, in the knowledge of Christ, in the love and image of God; and will do so, not only till death, but to all eternity.

Q. *How are we to wait for this change?*

A. Not in careless indifference or indolent inactivity, but in vigorous, universal obedience, in a zealous keeping of all the commandments, in watchfulness and painfulness, in denying ourselves and taking up our cross daily; as well as in earnest prayer and fasting and a close attendance on all the ordinances of God. And if any man dream of attaining it any other way (yea, or of keeping it when it is attained, when he has received it even in the largest measure), he deceive his own soul. It is true, we receive it by simple faith: But God does not, will not, give that faith unless we seek it with all diligence, in the way which He hath ordained.

25. It were well you should be thoroughly sensible of this—"the heaven of heavens is love." There is nothing higher in religion; there is, in effect, nothing else; if you look for anything but more love, you are looking wide of the mark, you are getting out of the royal way. And when you are asking others, "Have you received this or that

blessing?" if you mean anything but more love, you mean wrong; you are leading them out of the way, and putting them upon a false scent. Settle it then in your heart, that from the moment God has saved you from all sin, you are to aim at nothing more, but more of that love described in the thirteenth of the Corinthians. You can go no higher than this till you are carried into Abraham's bosom.

26. In the year 1764, upon a review of the whole subject, I wrote down the sum of what I had observed in the following short propositions:

(1) There is such a thing as perfection; for it is again and again mentioned in Scripture.

(2) It is not so early as justification; for justified persons are to "go on unto perfection" (Heb. 6:1).

(3) It is not so late as death; for St. Paul speaks of living men that were perfect (Phil. 3:15).

(4) It is not absolute. Absolute perfection belongs not to man, nor to angels, but to God alone.

(5) It does not make a man infallible: None is infallible while he remains in the body.

(6) Is it sinless? It is not worth while to contend for a term. It is "salvation from sin."

(7) It is "perfect love" (1 John 4:18). This is the essence of it; its properties, or inseparable fruits, are, rejoicing evermore, praying without ceasing, and in everything giving thanks (1 Thess. 5:16–18). 55

(8) It is improvable. It is so far from lying in an indivisible point,

from being incapable of increase, that one perfected in love may grow in grace far swifter than he did before.

(9) It is amissible, capable of being lost; of which we have numerous instances. But we were not thoroughly convinced of this, till five or six years ago.

(10) It is constantly both preceded and followed by a gradual work.

(11) But is it in itself instantaneous or not? In examining this, let us go on step by step.

An instantaneous change has been wrought in some believers: None can deny this.

Since that change, they enjoy perfect love; they feel this, and this alone; they "rejoice evermore, pray without ceasing, and in everything give thanks." Now, this is all that I mean by perfection; therefore, these are witnesses of the perfection which I preach.

"But in some this change was not instantaneous." They did not perceive the instant when it was wrought. It is often difficult to perceive the instant when a man dies; yet there is an instant in which life ceases. And if ever sin ceases, there must be a last moment of its existence, and a first moment of our deliverance from it.

"But if they have this love now, they will lose it." They may; but they need not. And whether they do or no, they have it now; they now experience what we teach. They now are all love; they now rejoice, pray, and praise without ceasing.

"However, sin is only suspended in them; it is not destroyed." Call it which you please. They are all love to-day; and they take no thought for the morrow.

"But this doctrine has been much abused." So has that of justification by faith. But that is no reason for giving up either this or any other scriptural doctrine. "When you wash your child," as one speaks, "throw away the water; but do not throw away the child."

"But those who think they are saved from sin say they have no need of the merits of Christ." They say just the contrary. Their language is, "Every moment, Lord, I want the merit of thy death!"

They never before had so deep, so unspeakable, a conviction of the need of Christ in all His offices as they have now.

Therefore, all our preachers should make a point of preaching perfection to believers constantly, strongly, and explicitly; and all believers should mind this one thing, and continually agonize for it.

JOHN WESLEY

CHARLES **WESLEY**

CHAPTER 6

O FOR A THOUSAND TONGUES TO SING
MY GREAT REDEEMER'S PRAISE,
THE GLORIES OF MY GOD AND KING,
THE TRIUMPHS OF HIS GRACE!

INTRODUCTION

Charles Wesley (1707–1788), the consummate songwriter of the movement of Methodism, may also bear the apt designation of the poet laureate of holiness. While much could be said along historical and biographical lines, it would be better read elsewhere. This brief account designs to explore the essence of the poet himself through some of his best-known verse.

Whether an awakening or assurance, the moment of conversion or a milestone crisis, something happened in Charles Wesley's heart on the Day of Pentecost, 1738. His first thirty years held immense physical and spiritual struggle. Weak from almost constant sickness, Charles wrote these words in his journal on that day:

SUN., MAY 21ST, 1738. I waked in hope and expectation of His coming. At nine my brother and some friends came, and sang an hymn to the Holy Ghost. My comfort and hope were hereby increased. In about half-an-hour they went: I betook myself to prayer; the substance as follows:

Oh Jesus, Thou hast said, "I will come unto you"; Thou hast said, "I will send the Comforter unto you"; Thou hast said, "My Father and I will come unto you, and make our abode with you." Thou art God who canst not lie; I wholly rely upon Thy most true promise: accomplish it in Thy time and manner.

Having said this, I was composing myself to sleep, in quietness and peace, when I heard one come in (Mrs. Musgrave, I thought, by the voice) and say, "In the name of Jesus of Nazareth, arise, and believe, and thou shalt be healed of all thy infirmities." I wondered how it should enter into her head to speak in that manner. The words struck me to the heart. I sighed, and said within myself, "O that Christ would but speak thus to me from Christ of my recovery, soul and body.

. . . I rose and looked into the Scripture. The words that first presented were, "And now, Lord, what is my hope? truly My hope is even in Thee." I then cast down my eye, and met, "He hath put a new song in my mouth, even a thanksgiving unto our God. Many shall see it, and fear, and shall put their trust in the Lord." Afterwards I opened upon Isaiah 40:1: "Comfort ye, comfort ye, my people, saith your God: speak ye comfortably to Jerusalem, and cry unto her, that her warfare is accomplished, that her iniquity is pardoned; for she hath received of the Lord's hand double for all her sin." I now found myself at peace with God, and rejoiced in hope of loving Christ. My temper for the rest of the day was mistrust of my own great, but before unknown, weakness. I saw that by faith I stood; by the continual support of faith, which kept me from falling, though of myself I am ever sinking into sin. I went to bed still sensible of my own weakness (I humbly hope to be more and more so), yet confident of Christ's pro'ection.

Fitting indeed that this storied poet of the Spirit should have such an encounter on a red-letter day like Pentecost. Though Charles wrote poems since age eight, something new of the Spirit entered his song, transforming his struggle into the very song of salvation. One of his most famous hymns, "Come, O Thou Traveller Unknown," though little sung today, captures this epic struggle for holiness so many have shared.

(verse 1)

Come, O thou Traveller unknown,
Whom still I hold, but cannot see!
My company before is gone,
And I am left alone with Thee;
With Thee all night I mean to stay,
And wrestle till the break of day.

(verse 2)

I need not tell Thee who I am,
My misery and sin declare;
Thyself hast called me by my name,
Look on Thy hands, and read it there;
But who, I ask Thee, who art Thou?
Tell me Thy name, and tell me now.

61

CHARLES WESLEY

(verse 10)

'Tis Love! 'tis Love! Thou diedst for me!

I hear Thy whisper in my heart;

The morning breaks, the shadows flee,

Pure, universal love Thou art;

To me, to all, Thy bowels move;

Thy nature and Thy Name is Love.

He wrote the poetry of the Spirit as the Son of God cauterized the wounds of holiness in his own life. In his hymns he shows us not so much holiness as the application of Scripture's principles but holiness as immersion in Scripture's story. Charles takes concepts such as justification by grace through faith and translates them into experientially singable stories. Through his craft, he teaches the central doctrine of our faith to dance, as evidenced in "Arise, My Soul, Arise."

(verse 1)

Arise, my soul, arise; shake off thy guilty fears;

The bleeding sacrifice in my behalf appears:

Before the throne my surety stands,

Before the throne my surety stands,

My name is written on His hands.

(verse 4)

The Father hears Him pray,

His dear anointed One;

He cannot turn away,

the presence of His Son;

His Spirit answers to the blood,

62

His Spirit answers to the blood,
And tells me I am born of God.

At the same time he wrote his own salvation story, he penned the poetry of a movement as the Spirit blazed revival throughout all of England. Consider what may fairly be called the anthem of holiness, the hymn, "And Can it Be?":

(verse 1)
And can it be that I should gain
An interest in the Savior's blood!
Died He for me, who caused his pain?
For me, who him to death pursued?
Amazing love! How can it be
That Thou, my God, shouldst die for me?
Amazing love! How can it be
That Thou, my God, shouldst die for me?

(verse 4)
Long my imprisoned sprit lay,
Fast bound in sin and nature's nig't;
Thine eye diffused a quickening ray;
I woke, the dungeon flamed with light;
My chains fell off, my heart was free,
I rose, went forth, and followed Thee.
My chains fell off, my heart was free,
I rose, went forth, and followed Thee.

CHARLES WESLEY

Charles Wesley's work reveals a poet who takes words to their highest powers. Like a chemist experimenting in the lab, he combined words into combusting compositions, blazing with the fire of holiness. While theologians laboriously wrestle with words to describe, define, and delineate the doctrines of salvation and character of God, the poet-theologian Wesley trained words to move in declaration of God's glory. Wesley shaped words into a mighty cathedral so profound that the Church can't stop singing them.

He lived life at the intersection of theology and experience, of story and song, and he showed us how songwriting impacts the larger theological controversies of the day. In the face of a doctrine damning millions to eternal hell without any option to choose Christ, Wesley sings of a Savior and salvation available to all. Sample the first two stanzas of the hymn, "Come, Sinners, to the Gospel Feast."

Come, sinners, to the Gospel feast;
Let every soul be Jesus' guest.
Ye need not one be left behind,
For God hath bid all humankind.

Sent by my Lord, on you I call;
The invitation is to all.
Come, all the world! Come, sinner, thou!
All things in Christ are ready now.

Not only did he sing of a salvation for all, but he demonstrated it through extraordinary ministry. Charles Wesley preached in the fields just as his brother did. He also spent considerable time ministering in prisons.

Plenteous He is in truth and grace;
He wills that all the fallen race
Should turn, repent, and live;
His pardoning grace for all is free;
Transgression, sin, iniquity,
He freely doth forgive.

Into an era despairing over depravity with an anemic understanding of sanctification, Wesley wrote of the glorious possibilities of Christian perfection and helped make accessible what had theretofore been largely lost in human experience. Consider this lesser known verse inspired by 1 Thessalonians 4:3:

He wills, that I should holy be:
That holiness I long to feel,
That full Divine conformity
To all my Saviour's righteous will:

See Lord, the travail of Thy soul
Accomplish'd in the change of mine,
And plunge me, every whit made whole,
In all the depths of love Divine.

And then that glorious, familiar anthem of the Church:

Love divine, all loves excelling,
Joy of heaven, to earth come down;
Fix in us Thy humble dwelling;
All Thy faithful mercies crown!

CHARLES WESLEY

Jesus, Thou art all compassion,
Pure, unbounded love Thou art;
Visit us with Thy salvation;
Enter every trembling heart.

Breathe, O breathe Thy loving Spirit
Into every troubled breast!
Let us all in Thee inherit;
Let us find that second rest.
Take away our bent to sinning;
Alpha and Omega be;
End of faith, as its beginning,
Set our hearts at liberty.

Come, Almighty to deliver,
Let us all Thy life receive;
Suddenly return and never,
Never more Thy temples leave.
Thee we would be always blessing,
Serve thee as Thy hosts above,
Pray and praise Thee without ceasing,
Glory in Thy perfect love.

Finish, then, Thy new creation;
Pure and spotless let us be.
Let us see Thy great salvation
Perfectly restored in Thee;
Changed from glory into glory,
Till in heaven we take our place,

Till we cast our crowns before Thee,
Lost in wonder, love, and praise.

For Wesley, holiness could not be captured by concepts and doctrines but only in the inexhaustible beauty of the holy one of God, Jesus Christ. In the final analysis, Jesus is the subject, object, and captivating grammar of his hymnody.

My heart is full of Christ, and longs
Its glorious matter to declare!
Of Him I make my loftier songs,
I cannot from His praise forbear;
My ready tongue makes haste to sing
The glories of my heavenly King.

From Advent to Christmas, Lent to Easter, Ascension to Pentecost and onward, Wesley teaches us to sing the story of Jesus with such glorious movement that holiness sweeps across the land like an unstoppable tide. Herein lies the secret power of poets and if not all books of the Bible, the Lord's Supper, the order of salvation, the Christian calendar, and beyond.

CHRISTMAS

Hark! the herald angels sing,
"Glory to the newborn King,
peace on earth, and mercy mild,
God and sinners reconciled!"
Joyful, all ye nations rise,

CHARLES WESLEY

join the triumph of the skies;
with th' ange'ic host proclaim,
"Christ is born in Bethlehem!"
Hark! the herald angels sing,
"Glory to the new born King!"

EASTER

Christ the Lord is risen today, Alleluia!
Earth and heaven in chorus say, Alleluia!
Raise your joys and triumphs high, Alleluia!
Sing, ye heavens, and earth reply, Alleluia!

Soar we now where Christ hath led, Alleluia!
Following our exalted Head, Alleluia!
Made like Him, like Him we rise, Alleluia!
Ours the cross, the grave, the skies, Alleluia!

PENTECOST

O Thou who camest from above,
the pure celestial fire to impart,
kindle a flame of sacred love
upon the mean altar of my heart.

There let it for Thy glory burn
with inextinguishable blaze,
and trembling to its source return,
in humble prayer and fervent praise.

In Charles Wesley's case, to become a student of the poetry will make one a friend of the poet. In his friendship, we cannot miss the glory of holiness: a God who meets us as sinners and transforms us into singers and saints. We end as we began, with verse 7 from one of the most sung songs in our faith, "O For a Thousand Tongues to Sing":

> *In Christ your Head, you then shall know,*
> *Shall feel your sins forgiven;*
> *Anticipate your heaven below,*
> *And own that love is heaven.*

—J. D. WALT

69

JOHN **FLETCHER**

CHAPTER 7

INTRODUCTION

The life stories of men such as John Fletcher (1729–1785) are at once both devastating and uplifting. They are devastating in their unflinching portrayal of holiness, and leave the reader grieved over his own comparative coldness of heart. Yet they are uplifting in their daring declaration of all that is possible in this life. But even among the elite, Fletcher was a rare breed. He was a man so gifted in the pulpit that John Wesley praised him as a superior preacher to George Whitefield, who is considered by many to be the finest orator of his generation. Yet his most striking characteristic is the humble demeanor that was his by virtue of his constant communion with his Heavenly Father. Here was a man with the heart of a saint and the tongue of a prophet, whose legacy we have ignored to our detriment.

Despite Wesley's urgings that he assume the life of a traveling preacher, Fletcher resigned himself to the anonymity of the local parish. From 1760 to 1785, virtually the full breadth of his ministry,

Fletcher served as vicar of Madeley. It's been told that the windows of the chapel had to be raised to accommodate the crowds that gathered outside to hear this homiletical mastermind. But Fletcher didn't just preach to his people. He prayed with them. He counseled them. And seeing how many of his parishioners toiled in the deplorable conditions of the local mines, Fletcher even found himself speaking out for workers' rights. Like many of his Methodist contemporaries, Fletcher was always more, but never less, than a social revolutionary. Yet above all he was or ever could have been, John Fletcher was a lover of God and a lover of people.

So much more could be said of this man. So much more needs to be said of this man. We could speak at length of his final years as a spouse to Mary Bosanquet Fletcher, a woman who by many accounts matched her husband in both piety and passion. We could speak of how beloved he was by John Wesley. Not only did Wesley hand-pick Fletcher to succeed him as the leader of the Methodist movement, but he also insisted on personally writing Fletcher's biography after the eminent pastor succumbed to a lengthy illness at the age of fifty-five. We could speak of what a wise old sage he would have been had he not lived his brief life with the rigidity of a desert monk. Yet I'm convinced that Fletcher would have been both baffled and embarrassed by such attention. And so, I will say this: The Christ in me leaps for joy when he sees the Christ in John Fletcher. In many ways, the Christ in me, being woefully neglected and untended, sees in John Fletcher the fullness of his potential.

Like John Wesley, John Fletcher was a prolific letter writer. What follows is a short sampling of his most heartfelt correspondence.

—Josh LeRoy

LETTERS OF FLETCHER

TO MISS HATTON

Dear Madam, I thank you for the letter of your correspondent. What he says about luminous joy may be the case in some of God's dear children. But I apprehend that God's design in withholding from them those gracious influences which work upon and melt the sensitive, affectionate part in the soul, is to put us more upon using the nobler powers—the understanding and the will. These are always more in the reach of a child of God, while the other greatly depend upon the texture of the animal frame. And if they are not stirred in a natural way, the Spirit of God can alone, without our concurrence in general, excite them. Therefore believe, love, take up your cross, and run after Jesus.

You must let friends and foes talk about your dress, while you mind only Jesus, His Word, and your own conscience. You talk of hearing me soon. I dare never invite anyone to hear me, though I am glad to see my friends. But now I can invite you with pleasure to come and hear a preacher who, under God, will make you amends for the trouble of a journey to Madeley. His name is M_____. He may possibly stay a Sunday or two more with me. But Jesus has promised to be always with His poor followers. To His merciful hand I commend both you and your unworthy friend.

ON LUKEWARMNESS

The lukewarm are of two sorts. The first will speak against enormities but plead for little sins—will go to church and sacrament, but also to plays, races, and shows—will read the Bible, and also romances and trifling books. They will have family prayer, at least on Sundays, but after it unprofitable talk, evil speaking, and worldly conversation. They plead for the church, yet leave it for a card party, a pot companion, or the fireside. They think they are *almost* good enough, and they who aim at being better are (to be sure) hypocrites. They are under the power of anger, evil desire, and anxious care. But they suppose that all men are the same, and talk much of being saved by true repentance and doing all they can. They undervalue Christ, extol morality and good works, and do next to none. They plead for old customs. They will do as their fathers did, though ever contrary to the word of God. Whatever hath not custom to plead for it, though ever so much recommended in Scripture, is accounted by them a heresy. They are greatly afraid of being too good, and making too much ado about their souls and eternity. They will be sober, but not enthusiasts. The scriptures they quote most and understand least are: "Be not righteous over much"; "God's mercies are over all His works"; "There is a time for all things"; etc. They call themselves by the name of Christ, but worship Baal.

The second sort of lukewarm persons assent to all the whole Bible, talk of repentance, faith, and the new birth, commend holiness, plead for religion, use the outward means, and profess to be and to do more than others. But they yield to carelessness, self-indulgence, fear of man, dread of reproach and of loss, hatred of the cross, love of ease, and the false pleasures of a vain imagination. These say, do, and really suffer many things; but they rest short of the true change of heart, the one thing needful being still lacking. They are as the foolish virgins, without oil—as the man not having on the wedding garment.

Of these the Lord hath said, "He will spew them out of His mouth." But why so severe a sentence? Because, (1) Christ will have man hearty and true to His principles. He looks for truth in the inward parts. As a consistent character, He commended even the unjust steward. (2) Religion admits of no lukewarmness, and it is by men of this character that His name is blasphemed. (3) A bad servant is worse than a careless neighbor; and a traitor in the guise of a friend is more hateful and more dangerous than an open enemy. Judas was more infamous than Pilate. (4) The cold having nothing to trust to, and harlots and publicans, enter into the Kingdom of Heaven before moral or evangelical Pharisees who, in different degrees, know their Master's will and do it not. "They shall be beaten with many stripes."

TO THE BRETHREN IN AND ABOUT MADELEY
NYON, FEB. 11TH 1779

My dear companions in tribulation—Peace and mercy, faith, hope, and love be multiplied to you all in general, and to each of you in particular, from the Father of mercies, through the Lord Jesus Christ, by the Spirit of grace. I thank you for your kind remembrance of me in your prayers. I am yet spared to pray for you. O that I had more power with God! I would bring down all Heaven into all hearts. Strive together in love for the living faith, the glorious hope, the sanctifying, perfecting love once delivered to the saints. Look to Jesus. Move on. Run yourselves in the heavenly race, and let each sweetly draw his brother along, till the whole company appears before the redeeming God in Zion, adorned as a bride for the heavenly Bridegroom.

I hope God will, in His mercy, spare me to see you in the flesh. And if I cannot labor for you, I shall gladly suffer with you. If you will put health into my flesh, marrow in my bones, joy in my heart, and life into my whole frame, be of one heart and of one soul. Count nothing your own but your sin and shame; and bury that dreadful property in the grave, the bottomless grave of our Savior. Let all you are and have be His that bought you, and His members, for His sake. Dig hard in the Gospel mines for hidden treasure. Blow hard the furnace of prayer with the bellows of faith, until you are melted into love, and the dross of sin is purged out of every heart. "There is a river that maketh glad the city of God." It is the grace that flows from His throne. Jesus is the vessel, the heavenly ark. Get together into Him, and sweetly sail down into the ocean of eternity. So shall you be true miners, furnace-men, and bargemen. Farewell in Jesus.

TO THE SOCIETIES IN AND ABOUT MADELEY

My dear brethren—Grace and peace, truth and love be multiplied unto you all. Stand fast in the Lord, my dear brethren. Stand fast to Jesus. Stand fast to one another. Stand fast to the vow we have so often renewed together upon our knees and at the Lord's table. Resolve to save yourselves altogether. Don't be so unloving, so cowardly, as to let one of your little company fall into the hands of the world and the devil. Agree to crucify the body of sin together.

I am still in a strait between the work which Providence cuts out for me here and the love which draws me to you. When I shall have the pleasure of seeing you, let it not be embittered by the sorrow of finding any of you half-hearted and lukewarm. Let me find you all strong in the Lord and increased in humble love. Solute from me all that followed with us fifteen years ago. Care still for your old brethren. Let there be no Cain among you, no Esau, no Lot's wife. Let the love of David and Jonathan, heightened by that of Martha, Mary, Lazarus, and our Lord, shine in all your thoughts, your tempers, your words, your looks, and your actions. If you love one another, your little meetings will be a renewed feast; and the God of love, who is peculiarly present where two or three are gathered together in the name of Jesus and in the Spirit of love, will abundantly bless you. Bear me still upon your breasts in prayer, as I do you upon mine; and rejoice with me that the Lord who made, redeemed, and comforts us, bears us all upon His. I am yours in Him.

77

JOHN FLETCHER

RICHARD **ALLEN**

CHAPTER **8**

INTRODUCTION

Born a slave on February 14, 1760, Richard Allen (1760–1831) would become one of the first black Methodist preachers in the United States and the founder of the African Methodist Episcopal Church. Allen's pursuit of personal and social holiness is reflected throughout his writing despite his constant battles with racial inequality, slavery, unpaid work, and conflicts with the church authorities of the time. The African Methodist Episcopal Church arose out of a quest for justice and a longing to worship the Lord.

At about age twenty, Allen experienced salvation and sanctification through Jesus Christ. His witness was so credible that his fellow slaves also accepted Christ. Allen continued to serve his unsaved slave owner faithfully and with a great work ethic. Convinced by Allen's superior integrity, the master eventually accepted Christ himself and allowed Allen to purchase his freedom.

Allen's autobiography describes his struggle of moving into mainstream society and his efforts at finding work. He eventually began preaching four to five times a day for the Methodist Connexion. When Allen's friend was forcibly removed from a white church in the middle of worship, Allen led the way in forming the first African church in the United States.

Ironically, one of Allen's greatest foes in this process was white church leadership. Allen had been part of a fairly enlightened white church that allowed blacks to worship in certain corners of the sanctuary. But when the African church started to worship separately, whites began to fear their loss of power. White leaders of the time liked "equality" as long as blacks did not become too powerful. They supported blacks in the church as long as whites still held the highest positions.

Other remarkable figures in this narrative are the "several respectable white citizens" who attended the African church. When the Methodist Connexion forcibly tried to take over the African church, these white citizens used their leveraging power for justice. Not only were they antislavery, but they actually participated in the formation of the black church. They submitted themselves to black leadership as an act of justice. And when strife occurred, these well-respected citizens used their position of privilege to negotiate with others who acted unjustly.

Allen's example of personal and social holiness is compelling. He shows us the kinds of things holiness calls us to. As we grow in holiness, we are unable to stay neutral. Holiness calls us to action. In particular, holiness calls us to action against injustice. Allen's move to separate black worship from white worship was needed in order to assert the dig-

80

nity and equality of black people. However, today, Christians have a different role to play. Today, holiness still compels us to seek racial justice. Holiness compels us to seek a kingdom manifestation of multiculturalism. Richard Allen's commitment to personal and social holiness is exemplary. As we seek personal and social holiness, we too will be compelled to be justice seekers, spokespersons for the underprivileged, and pursuers of God's kingdom on earth as it is in heaven.

—CHRISTY LIBSCOMB

PERSONAL WRITINGS

I was born in the year of our Lord 1760, on February 14th, a slave to Benjamin Chew, of Philadelphia. My mother and father and four children of us were sold into Delaware State, near Dover, and I was a child and lived with him until I was upwards of twenty years of age, during which time I was awakened and brought to see myself poor, wretched and undone, and without the mercy of God must be lost. Shortly after I obtained mercy through the blood of Christ, and was constrained to exhort my old companions to seek the Lord. I went rejoicing for several days, and was happy in the Lord, in conversing with many old experienced Christians. I was brought under doubts, and was tempted to believe I was deceived, and was constrained to seek the Lord afresh.... One night I thought hell would be my portion. I cried unto Him who delighteth to hear the prayers of a poor sinner;

RICHARD ALLEN

and all of a sudden my dungeon shook, my chains flew off, and glory to God, I cried. My soul was filled. I cried, enough for me—the Saviour died. Now my confidence was strengthened that the Lord, for Christ's sake, had heard my prayers, and pardoned all my sins. I was constrained to go from house to house, exhorting my old companions, and telling to all around what a dear Saviour I had found. I joined the Methodist society, and met in class at Benjamin Wells's, in the forest, Delaware State....

My master was an unconverted man, and all the family; but he was what the world called a good master. He was more like a father to his slaves than any thing else. He was a very tender, humane man.... Our neighbours, seeing that our master indulged us with the privilege of attending meeting once in two weeks, said that Stokeley's negroes would soon ruin him; and so my brother and myself held a council together that we would attend more faithfully to our master's business, so that it should not be said that religion made us worse servants, we would work night and day to get our crops forward, so that they should be disappointed. We frequently went to meeting on every other Thursday; but if we were likely to be backward with our crops we would refrain from going to meeting. When our master found we were making no provision to go to meeting, he would frequently ask us if it was not our meeting day, and if we were not going. We would frequently tell him, "No, sir, we would rather stay at home and get our work done." He would tell us, "Boys, I would rather you would go to your meeting: if I am not good myself, I like to see you striving yourselves to be good." Our reply would be, "Thank you, sir; but we would rather stay and get our crops forward." So we always continued to keep our crops more forward than our neighbours.... At length our master said he was convinced that religion made slaves better and not worse, and often boasted of his slaves for their honesty and industry.... [T]he class-leader (John Gray)...preached at my old master's house.... [A]t length Freeborn Garrison preached from these words, "Thou art weighed in the balance, and art found wanting." [M]y master believed himself to be one of that number, and after that he could not be satisfied to hold slaves, believing it to be wrong. And after that he proposed to me and my brother buying our times, to pay him sixty pounds gold and silver, or two thousand dollars continental money, which we complied with in the year 17–....

After peace was proclaimed I then travelled extensively, striving to preach the Gospel.... [I] preached on Sabbath day to a large congregation of different persuasions, and my dear Lord was with me.... Many souls were awakened, and cried aloud to the Lord to have mercy upon them.... I frequently preached twice a day, at 5 o'clock in the morning and in the evening, and it was not uncommon for me to preach from four to five times a day. I established prayer meetings; I raised a society in 1786 of forty-two members. I saw the necessity of erecting a place of worship for the coloured people.... Mr. W—— was much opposed to an African church, and used very degrading and insulting language to us, to try and prevent us from going on.... We felt ourselves much cramped; but my dear Lord was with us, and we believed, if it was His will the work would go on, and that we would be able to succeed in building the house of the Lord.

A number of us usually attended St. George's Church in Fourth street; and when the coloured people began to get numerous in attending the church, they moved us from the seats we usually sat on, and placed us around the wall, and on Sabbath morning we went to church

83

RICHARD ALLEN

and the sexton stood at the door, and told us to go in the gallery. He told us to go, and we would see where to sit. We expected to take the seats over the ones we formerly occupied below, not knowing any better. We took those seats. Meeting had begun, and they were nearly done singing, and just as we got to the seats, the elder said, "Let us pray." We had not been long upon our knees before I heard considerable scuffling and low talking. I raised my head up and saw one of the trustees, H—— M——, having hold of the Rev. Absalom Jones, pulling him up off of his knees, and saying, "You must get up—you must not kneel here." Mr. Jones replied, "Wait until prayer is over." Mr. H—— M—— said, "No, you must get up now, or I will call for aid and I force you away." Mr. Jones said, "Wait until prayer is over, and I will get up and trouble you no more." With that he beckoned to one of the other trustees, Mr. L—— S—— to come to his assistance. He came, and went to William White to pull him up. By this time prayer was over, and we all went out of the church in a body, and they were no more plagued with us in the church. This raised a great excitement and inquiry among the citizens, in so much that I believe they were ashamed of their conduct. But my dear Lord was with us, and we were filled with fresh vigour to get a house erected to worship God in.

Seeing our forlorn and distressed situation, many of the hearts of our citizens were moved to urge us forward.... [Dr. Benjamin Rush and Mr. Robert Ralston] pitied our situation, and subscribed largely towards the church, and were very friendly towards us, and advised us how to go on. We appointed Mr. Ralston our treasurer. Dr. Rush did much for us in public by his influence. I hope the name of Dr. Benjamin Rush and Mr. Robert Ralston will never be forgotten among us. They were the two first gentlemen who espoused the cause of the oppressed, and aided us in building the house of the Lord for the poor Africans to worship in. Here was the beginning and rise of the first African church in America.

[The Methodist elder] stationed in this city was such an opposer to our proceedings of erecting a place of worship, [he] would neither preach for us, nor have any thing to do with us. We then held an election, to know what religious denomination we should unite with. At the election it was determined—there were two in favour of the Methodist, the Rev. Absalom Jones and myself, and a large majority in favour of the Church of England. The majority carried. Notwithstanding we had been so violently persecuted by the elder, we were in favour of being attached to the Methodist connexion; for I was confident that there was no religious sect or denomination would suit the capacity of the coloured people as well as the Methodist; for the plain and simple gospel suits best for any people, for the unlearned can understand, and the learned are sure to understand.... The Methodists were the first people that brought glad tidings to the coloured people. I feel thankful that ever I heard a Methodist preach. We are beholden to the Methodists, under God, for the light of the Gospel we enjoy; for all other denominations preached so high-flown that we were not able to comprehend their doctrine....

In July, 1794, Bishop Asbury being in town I solicited him to open the church (this church will at present accommodate between 3 and 4000 persons) for us which he accepted. The Rev. John Dickins sung and prayed, and Bishop Asbury preached. The house was called Bethel.

85

RICHARD ALLEN

WILLIAM **WILBERFORCE**

CHAPTER 9

INTRODUCTION

More than two hundred years ago, a young man named William Wilberforce (1759–1833), through great ambition and religious conviction, changed the course of history. As part of the British Parliament, Wilberforce fought for justice and the rights of the millions of slaves who were being trafficked with brutal force in unequaled proportions. Wilberforce's political convictions rose not out of mere humanistic emotion or philosophy, but from the foundation of his religious beliefs.

Upon graduating from Cambridge University, he immediately entered into the political world. A few years later, through the ministry of the Methodists, Wilberforce found a personal and transformational relationship with Christ. He eventually associated himself with a group of evangelical Anglicans, specifically the Clapham sect of London.

His faith was not separated from his public life, for Wilberforce truly lived out his love for God and humanity. Nonetheless, his fight to abolish slavery in the British Empire did not come without its struggles and failures. For example, Wilberforce brought twelve resolutions to the British Parliament that would abolish the trade and trafficking of slaves. However, his first bill was defeated in 1791 by a vote of 163 to 88. A number of other failed attempts followed until his first success on February 23, 1807, when a resolution was passed that abolished the slave trade in the British West Indies, passing with a vote of 283 to 16. This bill abolished the trade of slaves but did not yet affect their legal status.

John Wesley was a contemporary—and likeminded activist—of Wilberforce's. Wesley taught that a scriptural Christian truly loves God, and through that love, truly loves man. He expressed these beliefs in his preaching and writing, including his famous abolitionist treatise published in 1774, "Thoughts Upon Slavery." This holiness message not only cries out for the physical well-being of each individual, but also for the eternal well-being of both the oppressed and the oppressor, the enslaved and the slave holder, the buyer and the seller, the powerless and powerful. Thus, Wilberforce's powerful message is best understood through the lens of the holiness message of John Wesley, which insists upon personal and societal change.

Influenced by holiness theology, Wilberforce brought his religious convictions into the political arena, providing an example for us today. The existence of human trafficking, refugee displacement, and immigrant abuse and misrepresentation remind us that the principles of holiness that propelled Wilberforce must influence us as well.

May the words that follow penetrate the mind, heart, and soul of every reader, and like Wilberforce, may we truly love others, which can only fully happen when we truly love God, the Creator and lover of all.

—JEREMY SUMMERS

THOUGHTS UPON SLAVERY

JOHN WESLEY

May I speak plainly to you? I must. Love constrains me; love to you, as well as to those you are concerned with. Is there a God? You know there is. Is He a just God? Then there must be a state of retribution; a state wherein the just God will reward every man according to his works. Then what reward will He render to you? . . .

Are you a man? Then you should have an human heart. But have you indeed? What is your heart made of? Is there no such principle as compassion there? Do you never feel another's pain? Have you no sympathy, no sense of human woe, no pity for the miserable?...

This equally concerns every merchant who is engaged in the slave-trade. It is you that induce the African villain to sell his countrymen; and in order thereto, to steal, rob, murder men, women, and children without number, by enabling the English villain to pay him for so doing, whom you overpay for his execrable labour. It is your money that is the spring of all, that empowers him to go on...

...And this equally concerns every gentleman that has an estate in our American plantations; yea, all slave-holders, of whatever rank and degree; seeing men-buyers are exactly on a level with men-stealers. Indeed you say, "I pay honestly for my goods; and I am not concerned to know how they are come by." Nay, but you are; you are deeply concerned to know they are honestly come by. Otherwise you are a partaker with a thief, and are not a jot honester than him. But you know they are not honestly come by.... Now, it is your money that pays the merchant, and through him the captain and the African butchers. You

WILLIAM WILBERFORCE

therefore are guilty, yea, principally guilty, of all these frauds, robberies, and murders. You are the spring that puts all the rest in motion.... O, whatever it costs, put a stop to its cry before it be too late: Instantly, at any price, were it the half of your goods, deliver thyself from blood-guiltiness! Thy hands, thy bed, thy furniture, thy house, thy lands, are at present stained with blood. Surely it is enough; accumulate no more guilt; spill no more the blood of the innocent! Do not hire another to shed blood; do not pay him for doing it! Whether you are a Christian or no, show yourself a man!...

Liberty is the right of every human creature, as soon as he breathes the vital air; and no human law can deprive him of that right which he derives from the law of nature....

If, therefore, you have any regard to justice (to say nothing of mercy, nor the revealed law of God), render unto all their due. Give liberty to whom liberty is due, that is, to every child of man, to every partaker of human nature.

John Wesley wrote the following letter—his last known letter—to Wilberforce, encouraging him to persevere and remember the reason for his fight in abolishing slavery.

February 24, 1791

Dear Sir: Unless the divine power has raised you up to be as *Athanasius contra mundum* [Athanasius against the world], I see not how you can go through your glorious enterprise in opposing that execrable villainy which is the scandal of religion, of England, and of human nature. Unless God has raised you up for this very thing, you will be worn out by the opposition of men and devils. But if God be for you, who can be against you? Are all of them together stronger than God? O be not weary of well doing! Go on, in the name of God and in the power of His might, till even American slavery (the vilest that ever saw the sun) shall vanish away before it.

Reading this morning a tract wrote by a poor African, I was particularly struck by that circumstance, that a man who has a black skin, being wronged or outraged by a white man, can have no redress; it being a *law* in all our Colonies that the *oath* of a black against a white goes for nothing. What villainy is this?

That He who has guided you from youth up may continue to strengthen you in this and all things is the prayer of, dear sir,

Your affectionate servant,

John Wesley

AN APPEAL TO THE RELIGION, JUSTICE, AND HUMANITY OF THE INHABITANTS OF THE BRITISH EMPIRE IN BEHALF OF THE NEGRO SLAVES IN THE WEST INDIES

WILLIAM WILBERFORCE

This cannot be surprising to any considerate mind. The Supreme Ordainer of all things, in His moral administration of the universe, usually renders crime in the way of natural consequences, productive of punishment; and it surely was to be expected that He would manifest, by some strong judicial sanction, His condemnation of practices which are at war with the marriage institution—the great expedient for maintaining the moral order and social happiness of mankind. . . .

In my estimate of things, however, and I trust in that of the bulk of my countrymen, though many of the physical evils of our colonial slavery are cruel and odious and pernicious, the almost universal des-

91

titution of religious and moral instruction among the slaves is the most serious of all the vices of the West Indian system; and had there been no other, this alone would have most powerfully enforced on my conscience the obligation of publicly declaring my decided conviction, that it is the duty of the legislature of this country to interpose for the mitigation and future termination of a state in which the ruin of the moral man, if I may so express myself, has been one of the sad consequences of his bondage.

It cannot be denied, I repeat, that the slaves, more especially the great body of the field Negroes, are practically strangers to the multiplied blessings of the Christian Revelation. . . .

May it not be from our having sinned in ignorance that we have so long been spared? But ignorance of a duty which we have had abundant means of knowing to be such, can by no one be deemed excusable. Let us not presume too far on the forbearance of the Almighty. Favoured in an equal degree with Christian light, with civil freedom, and with a greater measure of national blessings than perhaps any other country upon earth ever before enjoyed, what a return would it be for the goodness of the Almighty, if we were to continue to keep the descendants of the Africans, whom we have ourselves wrongfully planted in the western hemisphere, in their present state of unexampled darkness and degradation!

While efforts are making to rescue our country from this guilt and this reproach, let every one remember that he is answerable for any measure of assistance which Providence has enabled him to render towards the accomplishment of the good work. In a country in which the popular voice has a powerful and constitutional influence on the government and legislation, to be silent when there is a question of reforming abuses repugnant to justice and humanity is to share their guilt. Power always implies responsibility; and the possessor of it cannot innocently be neutral, when by his exertion moral good may be promoted, or evil lessened or removed. . . .

May I presume to interpose a word of caution to my fellow-laborers in this great cause? A caution which I can truly say I have ever wished myself to keep in remembrance, and observe in practice: it is, that while we expose and condemn the evils of the system itself, we should treat with and our and tenderness the characters of the West Indian proprietors. Let not the friends of the Africans forget that they themselves might have inherited West Indian property; and that, by early example and habit, they might have been subjected to the very prejudices which they now condemn. . . .

Let us act with energy suited to the importance of the interests for which we contend. Justice, humanity, and sound policy prescribe our course, and will animate our efforts. Stimulated by a consciousness of what we owe to the laws of God and the rights and happiness of man, our exertions will be ardent, and our perseverance invincible. Our ultimate success is sure; and ere long we shall rejoice in the consciousness of having delivered our country from greatest of her crimes, and rescued her character from the deepest stain of dishonour.

On July 26, 1833, three days before the death of William Wilberforce, the British Parliament passed the Slavery Abolition Act, which gave nearly one million slaves in the British Empire their freedom.

93

WILLIAM WILBERFORCE

ORANGE **SCOTT**

AND

LUTHER **LEE**

CHAPTER 10

INTRODUCTION

In 1842 slavery was the overriding issue in America. Congress was juggling the admission of slave states and free states to the Union, hoping to compromise its way to peace. The nation was literally and precisely half-slave and half-free in terms of the status of its states, a precarious balancing act that had been the law of the land since the Missouri Compromise of 1820. Slavery dominated the agenda of Congress and the conversations of most Americans.

But the churches were strangely silent. Methodism, which at the time was the largest denomination in the country, didn't want to risk losing the South. The same was true for Baptists, Presbyterians, and almost everyone else. Abolitionism was a growing force in America, but aside from the Quakers and the Mennonites, it had received virtually no official encouragement or support from the churches.

The situation began to change in the winter of 1842. Five prominent ministers withdrew from The Methodist Church in protest over their denomination's silence on slavery, a silence they saw as betrayal not only of scriptural principles and basic human rights but also of John Wesley's own example of outspoken opposition to slavery barely fifty years before. There was no doubt in their minds where the father of Methodism would stand on this issue, and so they chose to call themselves Wesleyan Methodists. They published a paper to explain their views, and lest anyone miss their point, they named it *The True Wesleyan.*

Orange Scott (1800–1841), who is considered to be the founder of the new church, was the first editor of its paper. As a presiding elder in New England, a responsibility second only to the office of bishop in the Methodist system, Scott had clashed repeatedly with the bishops over their heavy-handed attempts to squelch abolitionist sentiment in the denomination. He became an advisor to William Lloyd Garrison, America's most widely known abolitionist, and historian Donald Mathews of Princeton and the University of North Carolina has called Scott one of America's strongest antislavery voices.

After two years as editor, Scott was succeeded by Luther Lee (1800–1889), a Methodist theologian of note and another of the band of five who had formed the new denomination. Nicknamed "Logical Lee," he articulated the positions of the Wesleyan Methodists on theological, ecclesiastical, and moral issues with clarity and force. In 1853 Lee would preach the ordination sermon for Antoinette Brown, the first woman ordained to the Christian ministry.

Wesleyan Methodism was, in the memorable words of Orange Scott, "anti-slavery, anti-intemperance, anti-everything wrong," and yet it did not define itself solely by what it opposed. It was strongly pro-holiness. In fact, in 1844 Wesleyan Methodism became the first church to adopt a formal statement on sanctification as an article of religion in its book of discipline. Not even The Methodist Church had done that.

Social reform and Christian perfection went hand in hand for the Wesleyan Methodists. As Associate Editor Jotham Horton would write in the fourth issue of *The True Wesleyan*, "professed holiness," which can pass by men and women stripped of human rights and dignity without stopping to help, is not biblical holiness at all. "Holiness is not an abstraction," he wrote. "It is a living, loving, active principle. It is eminently practical."

For those first Wesleyan Methodists, social justice in the name of Christ was holiness in action. These excerpts from the pages of their periodical are not an exposition of holiness but an example of the application of holiness to real-world issues.

—BOB BLACK

THE TRUE WESLEYAN

EXCERPTS FROM THE INAUGURAL ISSUE, JANUARY 7, 1843

With the date of this communication closes our connection with the Methodist Episcopal Church. We take this step after years of consideration, and with a solemn sense of our responsibility to God. We take it with a view to his glory and the salvation of souls.

Twenty years and upwards of the best part of our lives has been spent in the service of this church, during which time we have formed

ORANGE SCOTT AND LUTHER LEE

acquaintances which have endeared to our hearts multitudes of Christian friends. Many of these are true kindred spirits, and we leave them with reluctance. But the view we take of our responsibility is not local in its bearings, nor limited in its duration. While we live, and when we die, we wish to bear a testimony which shall run parallel with coming ages; nay, with the annals of eternity. Many considerations of friendship as well as our temporal interests bind us to the church of our early choice. But for the sake of a high and holy cause, we can forego all these.

The M. E. Church is not only a slave-holding but a slavery-defending church. . . . She has said through some of her annual conferences that slavery is *not* a moral evil, while she has repeatedly refused, through her bishops, to allow other annual conferences to express the opposite sentiment. . . . Is there any prospect that this church will ever be reformed, so long as slavery exists in the country? . . .

The real moral reforms of the age, though in a sense subordinate to vital godliness, are nevertheless so closely allied to it that the advancement of the latter is essential to the progress of the former. They are but the application of Christian truth to existing evils. . . .

We intend . . . that the subject of Christian holiness, as taught by our standard writers and embodied in the experience of early Methodists, shall have suitable place and space in our columns. We rejoice to know that at present this work is advancing to a remarkable degree, both among ourselves and others. Many have recently experienced its fullness and are its living exemplifications, both in word and deed. This is ominous of great good, both to the church and the world. . . .

98   If ever there was an age and a place which required sound minds, pure hearts, and disinterested efforts, that age is the present—that

place is our own beloved country. It is with the benevolent, the philanthropic, the pious, to say, under God, what shall be the future character, happiness, and destiny of this nation. . . . We step into the breach to struggle with the various gigantic forms of oppression and vice now threatening to undermine man's most valued interests. Duty is ours—consequences, God's.

FROM THE FOURTH ISSUE, JANUARY 28, 1843

Holiness, doctrinally and experientially, is a subject of vital importance to the Christian. His usefulness and happiness are inseparable from a correct understanding and a cordial embrace of it, as taught in the Scriptures. This embrace implies the yielding of the whole heart, rather the whole man, body, soul, and spirit, to its entire control. . . .

It is most manifest that in this state the mind must possess a clear perception of moral distinctions. The wrongs of earth, and the woes consequent upon those wrongs, make an affecting appeal to the heart. It cannot be otherwise. . . .

That professed holiness which expends itself in personal comforts . . . which can pass by humanity despoiled of all its divinely endowed rights—suffering, degraded, down-trodden—and plead as its excuse that laws, civil and ecclesiastical even, authorize those wrongs, we believe is essentially wanting. . . . Can such persons possess holiness of heart, while to human appearance they are deaf to the groans of suffering humanity? Holiness is not an abstraction. It is not confined within the limits of church homilies, doctrinal, or even biblical phrases. It is a living, loving, active principle. It is eminently practical. Man can as easily stifle the fires of Etna or Vesuvius as quench the devout and woe-ameliorating ardors of holy love.

99

In the November 13, 1847, issue, editor Luther Lee printed the first of what would become a series of long letters from "Rev. A. Crooks of Guilford Circuit, North Carolina." The True Wesleyan *became the public voice of Adam Crooks and the Wesleyan pastors who followed him to the South as abolitionist ministers in the turbulent years before the Civil War. In this letter Crooks described his journey from Ohio to North Carolina to pastor an antislavery congregation in a slave-holding state. The letter was bracketed with these words.*

. . . I turned my face to go to the far South, to pronounce that Gospel which proclaims liberty to the captive and the opening of the prisons to them that are bound. . . . And now, at the commencement of my labors, let me call upon the whole church, and every lover of God and friend of man, to send up their earnest, faithful, importunate, and prevailing prayers that heaven would smile propitiously upon the cause in North Carolina; the good of our common Christianity and common country, the sacred demands of the trembling, weeping, bleeding, perishing slave, and the high and holy claims of the Holy One require it; yea, and future posterity will say Amen.

The True Wesleyan *regularly printed reports from the South over the next several years. In an August 9, 1851, letter to the editor, Crooks related his arrest weeks earlier when he was dragged by a mob from the pulpit of Lovejoy Chapel, a Wesleyan church named for a Presbyterian minister and abolitionist editor whose murder in 1837 gave the abolitionist cause its first nationally known martyr. This excerpt is a verbatim of an exchange between Crooks and a slave-holding magistrate named Luther, one of the leaders of the mob, as it appeared on the pages of* The True Wesleyan.

(L.) Those who have taken you have done God service.

(C.) Our Savior has told us that the time would come when those who kill his followers would think they did God service. But that question will be settled at the judgment, and the Judge will consider treatment to His servants as done unto Him. Now if He were on earth again, would you drive Him from the county?

(L.) I don't know what we might do, if He were an abolitionist.

A friend of Crooks wrote The True Wesleyan *to describe the conditions in his jail cell.*

The room in which the preacher was confined is about 9 by 13, and 7 to the ceiling above. His fare, or more properly his *foul*, was for bedding some blankets directly from the dungeon which were ponderous with dust, and so offensive as to be sickening; these spread upon the floor. His portion was two meals per day: breakfast and dinner. The food was passable, the floor was his table, his finger served instead of a fork, and pocket-knife for a table knife; a plate and bowl were his dishes. . . . A committee was appointed to read any and all writings which passed between him and his friends, who were not permitted to visit him. None but his enemies could enter that *sanctum sanctorum.*

Crooks was not released until he agreed to leave the county. He did not leave the state, however, and, along with his colleagues, continued 101 *to preach effectively and to operate at least one station on the*

Underground Railroad. During his four years in North Carolina he was poisoned twice; he survived both attacks but suffered lingering effects that would shorten his life. He also escaped an ambush laid for him one night on a country road. Eventually Crooks was forced from North Carolina by political and judicial authorities and reluctantly returned to Ohio, where he pastored. Others took his place in the South. In 1864 Crooks was elected editor of the paper to which he had contributed his stirring reports from the front lines of the antislavery struggle. He would lead the paper, then known as The American Wesleyan, *until his death ten years later at the age of fifty. He championed many causes as editor, among them the temperance movement and women's rights, because, like Orange Scott and Luther Lee before him, he saw moral reform as applied holiness. In his first editorial he wrote the following:*

The primal object of *The American Wesleyan* should be the success of Christian enterprise—"the spread of scriptural holiness over these lands"—consisting in piety and purity, correct faith, genuine experience, and corresponding practice. "Holiness unto the Lord" should radiate from every issue.

It did.

PHOEBE **PALMER**

CHAPTER 11

INTRODUCTION

There is an old German proverb that says: "pastor's children and miller's cows / turn out badly, furrow brows."

I have furrowed many a brow during my career as a PK.

The preacher in my household was my mother, Mabel Velva Boggs, an ordained minister in the Pilgrim Holiness Church. Brought up a strict Methodist in the hills of southeastern West Virginia, at seventeen she was converted while standing in a parking lot after attending a revival meeting held by a visiting Pilgrim Holiness evangelist. The second oldest of seven surviving children (five died in childhood), her father ("G.L.") insisted that she attend church with the rest of the family and continue her piano playing and leadership in the Epworth League. She responded by defying her father, and after a year of spiritual warfare, her stubborn witness led to the entire Boggs household moving en masse to join a new Pilgrim Holiness church plant.

Without graduating from high school, Mother enrolled at God's Bible School in Cincinnati. She came under the influence of a faculty member who left after a year to teach at Allentown Bible School. She followed him there and began her theological training in earnest. But the more she studied, the more she doubted her faith and even her salvation. After a two-year dark night/dry-well spell, she came to a point where, in her words, she either had to "lay it all on the altar" or leave school.

When she did lay it down, as we heard many times over, Mabel Velva Boggs had an experience of entire sanctification and began living the "way of holiness" and full salvation. The very act of laying down everything she held dear gave her the power to pick up a life of doing the very things she had "laid down": church planting, home mission work, musical evangelism, the dream of foreign missions work, and marriage. While working in the blueprint room of the shipyard at Newport News (Virginia), she helped start a new church at Norfolk and conducted revival meetings throughout Virginia, West Virginia, and North Carolina.

In 1945 Mother was speaking "Five Words from the Lord" at a revival meeting in Newport News, Virginia. That evening the Spirit descended on those assembled in a special way, and a backsliding Free-Methodist soldier by the name of Leonard Lucius Sweet found his heart "strangely warmed," both by the Spirit and by the preacher.

Her new ministry became the raising of her three sons in the "ways of holiness." What was most important to Mother was that "her boys" were being steeped in the Scriptures. We attended prayer meeting every Wednesday evening. And beginning at age five, we had to deal with Mother's memorization requirement: a new Bible verse every day during the school year. We could never accuse Mother of hypocrisy—her Bible was an appendage of her body. When you read the Bible, Mother insisted, it is God, the very God of very God, who is speaking to you through these words. That's why we learned to test our experience by the Scriptures; we don't test the Scriptures by our experience.

It seemed like we had in our nine-hundred-square-foot house everything John Wesley and John Bunyan wrote. Susanna Wesley was Mother's hero and role model. In fact, Mother raised us in the company of women: Deborah ("If the Lord couldn't find a man, he used a woman"), Rahab (we didn't learn she was a prostitute until our teens), Miriam, Lydia, Junia (Mother's "mystery woman"), Madame Guyon (surely a biblical writer, I thought, Mother quoted her so much), and Phoebe.

Who was Phoebe? I was never sure. Sometimes her name seemed to be linked with Paul and the book of Romans. But other times Phoebe went with someone else, a fuzzy figure who wrote books and hymns, had "parlor prayer meetings" like we had "family prayer meetings," and talked about the "latter rain." Most of all, Phoebe's metaphor of "the altar" was the centering fact of our existence.

Only in college would I learn that this second Phoebe was Phoebe Palmer (1807–1874), the most important woman theologian in the Protestant experience before our time. Before I ever read *The Promise of the Father* or *The Way of Holiness*, I knew her theology. I lived it.

Phoebe Palmer is widely known as the "Mother of the Holiness Movement" in America. She and her husband were profoundly influenced after reading the writings of John Wesley and began to preach the message of entire sanctification widely. She led what were called the "Tuesday Meetings for the Promotion of Holiness." These meet- ings initially were designed for women only, but her teaching became so popular that the meetings soon brought in many prominent men, including ministers and bishops. While some of her theology on Christian Perfection is considered controversial, there is no denying the impact of this fiery preacher on the message and the movement known as "holiness." Featured here is a brief selection from her classic work, *The Way of Holiness*.

—Leonard Sweet

THE WAY OF HOLINESS

IS THERE NOT A SHORTER WAY?

"I have thought," said one of the children of Zion to the other, as in love they journeyed onward in the way cast up for the ransomed of the Lord to walk in; "I have thought," said he, "whether there is not a *shorter way* of getting into this way of holiness than some of our brethren apprehend?"

"Yes," said the sister addressed, who was a member of the denomination alluded to; "Yes, brother, THERE IS A SHORTER WAY! O! I am sure this long waiting and struggling with the powers of darkness is not necessary. There is a shorter way." And then, with a solemn feeling of responsibility, and with a realizing conviction of the truth uttered, she added, "But, brother, there is but one way."

108   Days and even weeks elapsed, and yet the question, with solemn bearing, rested upon the mind of that sister. She thought of the affir-

mative given in answer to the inquiry of the brother—examined yet more closely the Scriptural foundation upon which the truth of the affirmation rested—and the result of the investigation tended to add still greater confirmation to the belief, that many sincere disciples of Jesus, by various needless perplexities, consume much time in endeavoring to get into this way, which might, more advantageously to themselves and others, be employed in making progress in it, and testifying, from experimental knowledge, of its blessedness.

How many, whom Infinite Love would long since have brought into this state, instead of seeking to be brought into the possession of the blessing at once, are seeking a preparation for the reception of it! They feel that their *convictions* are not deep enough to warrant an approach to the throne of grace, with the confident expectation of receiving the blessing *now*. Just at this point some may have been lingering months and years. Thus did the sister, who so confidently affirmed "there is a shorter way." And here, dear child of Jesus, permit the writer to tell you just how that sister found the "shorter way."

On looking at the requirements of the word of God, she beheld the command, "Be ye holy." She then began to say in her heart, "Whatever my former deficiencies may have been, God requires that I should *now* be holy. Whether *convicted*, or otherwise, *duty is plain.* God requires *present* holiness." On coming to this point, she at once apprehended a simple truth before unthought of, i.e., *Knowledge is conviction.* She well knew that, for a long time, she had been assured that God required holiness. But she had never deemed this knowledge a sufficient plea to take to God—and because of present need, to ask a present 109 bestowment of the gift.

Convinced that in this respect she had mistaken the path, she now, with renewed energy, began to make use of the knowledge already received, and to discern a "shorter way."

Another difficulty by which her course had been delayed she found to be here. She had been accustomed to look at the blessing of holiness as such a high attainment, that her general habit of soul inclined her to think it almost beyond her reach. This erroneous impression rather influenced her to rest the matter thus: "I will let every high state of grace, in name, alone, and seek only to be *fully conformed to the will of God, as recorded in his written word*. My chief endeavors shall be centered in the aim to be an humble *Bible Christian*. By the grace of God, all my energies shall be directed to this one point. With this single aim, I will journey onward, even though my faith may be tried to the uttermost by those manifestations being withheld, which have previously been regarded as essential for the establishment of faith."

On arriving at this point, she was enabled to gain yet clearer insight into the simplicity of the way. And it was by this process, after having taken the Bible as the rule of life, instead of the opinions and experience of professors, she found, on taking the blessed word more closely to the companionship of her heart, that no one declaration spoke more appealingly to her understanding than this: "Ye are not your own, ye are bought with a price, therefore glorify God in your body, and your spirit, which are his."

By this she perceived the duty of *entire consecration* in a stronger light, and as more sacredly blinding, than ever before. Here she saw God as her Redeemer, claiming, by virtue of the great price paid for the redemption of body, soul, and spirit, the *present and entire service* of all these redeemed powers.

By this she saw that if she lived constantly in the entire surrender of all that had been thus dearly purchased unto God, she was but an unprofitable servant; and that, if less than was rendered, she was worse than unprofitable, inasmuch as she would be guilty of keeping back part of that price which had been purchased unto God: "Not with corruptible things, such as silver and gold, but by the precious blood of Jesus." And after so clearly discerning the will of God concerning her, she felt that the sin of Ananias and Sapphira would be less culpable in the sight of Heaven than her own, should she not at once resolve on living in the *entire* consecration of all her redeemed powers to God.

Deeply conscious of past unfaithfulness, she now determined that the time past should suffice; and with a humility of spirit, induced by a consciousness of not having lived in the performance of such a "reasonable service," she was enabled, through grace, to resolve, with firmness of purpose, that entire devotion of heart and life to God should be the absorbing subject of the succeeding pilgrimage of life.

PHOEBE PALMER

B. T. **ROBERTS**

CHAPTER 12

INTRODUCTION

Recently, a high school student asked me, "Did Jesus ever spend money?" Many people think that the life Jesus lived was so foreign to us today that we simply cannot relate to it. It struck me that he had relegated Jesus to a different world than the one in which we live. We know that Jesus lived in a fairly economically advanced society. In a Roman-dominated reality, currency exchange was needed to function. Even more than this, we know economy also played a significant part in the landscape of Jewish worship in the Temple.

When do we see Jesus the angriest? John gives us a stunning picture of our Savior. Imagine in your mind's eye Jesus doing this: "So he made a whip out of cords, and drove all from the temple area, both sheep and cattle; he scattered the coins of the money changers and overturned their tables" (John 2:15).

One could argue that this drove Jesus' anger more than any other event we see recorded in Scripture. There is no question that Jesus confronted in His culture the same wrong those before him confronted and that you and I confront today: a lack of impartiality (treating people differently according to what they have). This injustice is what drove his anger in the Temple.

It is so easy to fall into the trap of believing that the Kingdom *needs* the resources of the rich to advance the cause of Christ. Clearly, God doesn't need the rich and powerful to accomplish His will. On the other hand, He can and does use *all* people, both rich and poor. From the Old Testament patriarch Abraham to New Testament Nicodemus, a member of the ruling council Sanhedrin, God has used affluent people to do His work. We can be led to believe through study of His life that even Jesus' ministry relied upon the financial resources of others. Throughout Scripture and even today, from the richest to the poorest, God will use anyone willing to offer what he or she has been entrusted with to build His Kingdom.

Regardless of our resources, we are all truly equal under the banner of Christ. Holy living demands that we must not treat our fellow human beings unequally according to their economic worth. When it comes to our wealth, none is more important than another before God. The holiness attribute of impartiality reminds us that all people hold equal value in the Lord's sight. And if we are to be a Church that is holy before God, we must share this same vision of our fellow Image-bearers.

B. T. Roberts (1823–1893), one of the founders of the Free Methodist Church, was passionate about this truth. In his classic work, *Holiness Teachings*, he said, "An individual who is holy cannot consistently belong to a Church that despises the poor." This belief translated into clear action, as he took strong stands against slavery, and the Methodist Church's practice of "pew rentals," which showed preference for the rich and prestigious. Such stands led to his expulsion from the Methodist

Episcopal Church, and to the formation of the "Free" Methodist Church in 1860. His legacy includes work for the rights of women, support of fair labor, and the founding of what is now Roberts Wesleyan College.

—JEFF ECKHART

HOLINESS TEACHINGS

CHAPTER XI: "ATTRIBUTES OF HOLINESS—IMPARTIALITY"

God is no respecter of persons. This does not mean that He regards the righteous and the wicked with the same degree of favor. But it does mean that He loves a poor man who is truly pious, just as much as He does a millionaire or a king who serves Him no better. In the ranks of an army, in time of war, are men from every position in life; but there are for all the same duties and the same dangers. The road to preferment is open to all alike. What is true, in theory at least, in the army, is true in fact in the Church of Jesus Christ. The same spirit of obedience and self-renunciation is required of all. "So whosoever of you he be, that forsaketh not all that he hath, he cannot be my disciple" (Luke 14:3).

In proportion as we become holy we become partakers of the mind that was in Christ. A holy person will not claim and accept any privilege in the house of God which is conceded to him on account of his wealth, but is denied to his poor but equally deserving brother. To him there is a depth of meaning in the words of our Saviour: "How can ye

115

believe which receive honor one of another, and seek not the honor that cometh from God only?" (John 5:44).

He is "a companion"—an equal—"of all them that fear God" (Ps. 119:6), and he does not accept any honor bestowed upon him on account of the superior worldly advantages he may enjoy.

Consequently a holy person should not buy or rent a seat in a house of worship. To do this would be to give his sanction to a practice which shuts the poor out of the house of God, and which introduces into the Church an aristocracy based on money.

Christ says, "The poor have the Gospel preached to them" (Matt. 11:5).

This is the standing miracle of the Gospel. False religions seek their votaries among the rich and powerful. The Gospel was made for the poor. It is adapted to their capacities and their wants. If the rich receive it they must come down to a level with the poor. They must lay aside their "gold and pearls and costly array" and be clothed upon with humility. In all ages the greatest triumphs of the Gospel have been won among the poor. Paul, writing to the saints at Corinth, one of the proudest cities of his times, said, "Ye see your calling; brethren, how that not many wise men after the flesh, not many mighty, not many noble are called; but God hath chosen the foolish things of the world to confound the wise; and God hath chosen the weak things of the world to confound the things which are mighty; and base things of the world, and things which are despised hath God chosen, yea, and things which are not, to bring to nought things that are" (1 Cor. 1:26–28).

John Wesley commenced his wonderful career among the poor, and his followers were mainly of this class. Were the churches holy, their houses of worship would be open for the poor just as freely as for the rich, and there would be one communion for all; as there is one

116

God and Father of us. An individual who is holy cannot consistently belong to a Church that despises the poor. But if grading a congregation according to its wealth—giving to the one, who is able and willing to pay the most, the best seat, irrespective of his Christian, or even moral character, and giving the poor seats by themselves, is not manifesting contempt for the poor, we know not how it can be manifested in the house of God. True holiness would correct all this. It honors those whom God honors. It would make trouble, for those professing holiness, to refuse to give their sanction to the selling of the right to hear the Gospel. But this is the nature of holiness—to make trouble wherever it comes in contact with sin. Light has no communion with darkness, and where one prevails it is to the exclusion of the other.

God has nowhere promised that holy men should enjoy exemption from troubles. But they are promised a final and glorious deliverance.

If you steadfastly refuse to show respect of persons in judgment, you may bring upon yourself persecution; but in no other way can you keep clear in your soul. There is a sterling integrity about holiness, which refuses to be swerved from righteous judgment by any apprehension of danger or expectation of reward. It chooses to "suffer affliction with the people of God, rather than to enjoy the pleasures of sin for a season" (Heb. 11:25).

Job says, "The cause which I knew not I searched out." He did not accept the popular voice as his verdict. He examined carefully, weighed impartially the evidence, and gave a just decision. "Thou shalt not respect the person of the poor, nor honor the person of the mighty: but in righteousness shalt thou judge thy neighbor" (Lev. 19:15).

117

CATHERINE **BOOTH**

CHAPTER 13

INTRODUCTION

During my college days I celebrated the Christmas season playing a pump organ on the streets of Cincinnati for the Salvation Army Christmas offerings. My daily part-time job was in the medical records office of a Salvation Army Hospital, and in the summers the staff invited me to live in one of the rooms of a large home that had been donated to the Salvation Army. Sadly, during those days I was unaware of the spectacular intellect and spiritual giant embodied in Catherine Booth (1829–1890).

Some ten years later, as my husband and I traveled by car, I read aloud a research paper written by Don and Lucille Sider Dayton titled "Women in the Holiness Movement." While reading of the life of Catherine Booth I became overwhelmed with emotion. In fact, I frequently had to wipe tears from my eyes so I could see the next sentence. Frankly, I was surprised at my emotional response. But then I began to realize, here was a mentor and model of the past.

Catherine's desire to know God, and her ability to honestly search for him, quickened my spirit. Her boldness to reach a broken world—from the teeming poor in the streets of London to the wealthy, intellectuals, and even royalty of Great Britain—reflected her belief that sanctification was more than a life lived in isolation. This life demanded a response to bring the cleansing power of God to all aspects of society. She described her final understanding of sanctification as "simple reception of Christ as an all-sufficient Savior, dwelling in my heart."

Reading the life of Catherine Booth during the road trip coincided with my personal journey. At that time I was working with the urban poor as well as involved in seeking systemic justice. At the same time I was attempting to integrate this work with my faith.

Here in Catherine's life I found the integration of holiness, social justice, and evangelism, as well as a love and dedication to family. Booth Tucker, her son-in-law biographer, declared, "One half of her mission consisted in resurrecting the buried talents of her sex, and the other half in humanizing. . . the spiritual in bringing religion out of the vague . . . into the area of practical politics."

When Catherine died, all of England mourned and fifty thousand people filed past her coffin. Her funeral was a grand celebration of a life fully devoted to her Lord and Savior Jesus Christ. Tens of thousands of voices joined in singing Isaac Watts' "When I Survey the Wondrous Cross." The service concluded with an invitation to all who would make a "whole-hearted surrender to God" by rising to their feet. Hundreds stood as the immense crowd sang,

Just as I am, Thou wilt receive,

Wilt welcome, pardon, cleanse, relieve,

Because Thy promise I believe
O Lamb of God, I come!

Yes, Catherine Booth is a model, but her life always points me to our Lord and Savior Jesus Christ.

—Jo Anne Lyon

SELECTIONS FROM "WOMAN'S RIGHT TO PREACH THE GOSPEL" AND OTHER WRITINGS

A LETTER, AUTUMN, 1859

"I hope he will wait a bit till I am stronger. If he does bring out any more in the same style, I rather think of going to Sunderland and delivering an address in answer to him. William says I should get a crowded house. I really think I shall try. . . . William is always pestering me to begin giving lectures and certainly this would be a good subject to start with. I am determined it shall not go unanswered."

So were the determined words of Catherine Booth written in one of her weekly letters in the autumn of 1859. Her indignation was roused by the Rev. Arthur Rees, who had just written a pamphlet attacking woman's right to preach. This pamphlet had been directed specifically against Mrs. Phoebe Palmer, who was then in Newcastle, England, conducting a series of meetings. Catherine much admired

Dr. and Mrs. Palmer's ministry and decided in favor of not waiting till she should be able to reply by a lecture but instead began writing her response. "This pamphlet has been a great undertaking for me," she wrote in a letter home from the seaside, where she had taken her ailing son Ballington, "and is much longer than I at first intended, being thirty-two pages. But when William came home and heard what I had written, he was very pleased with it, and urged me to proceed and not tie myself for space, but to deal thoroughly with the subject, and make it a tract on the subject of female teaching which would survive this controversy. . . . Whatever it is, it is my own . . . for I could get no help from any quarter. . . . William has done nothing but copy for me."

EXCERPTS FROM "WOMAN'S RIGHT TO PREACH THE GOSPEL"

Making allowance for the novelty of the thing, we cannot discover anything either unnatural or immodest in a Christian woman, becomingly attired, appearing on a platform or in a pulpit. By nature she seems fitted to grace either. . . .

Why should woman be confined exclusively to the kitchen and the distaff, anymore than man to the field and workshop? Did not God, and has not nature, assigned to man his sphere of labour, "to till the ground and to dress it"? And, if exemption from this kind of toil is claimed for a portion of the male sex, on the ground of their possessing ability for intellectual and moral pursuits, we must be allowed to claim the same privilege for woman; nor can we see the exception more unnatural in the one case than in the other, or why God in this solitary instance has endowed a being with powers which He never intended her to employ.

She goes on to deal with the perceived Scriptural prohibitions and gives proof of women as preachers and deacons in the early church. In addition she takes the opening chapters of Acts as the basis for her arguments: "We are in the first of these passages expressly told that the women were assembled with the disciples on the day of Pentecost; and in the second, that the cloven tongues sat upon them *each*, and the Holy Ghost filled them *all*, and they spake as the Spirit gave them utterance."

Catherine wrote these words as she was preparing for the birth of her fourth child. Interestingly enough, she did not write to defend herself. At that time she did not sense any "call" to preach but knew that those who were called, such as Mrs. Palmer and others, had the God-given right to obey. She argued that not all women are required to preach any more than all men are required to preach.

OTHER WRITINGS AND SPEECHES

As Catherine lay nursing her child, she felt her joy to be almost perfect. She was happy in a deep, thrilling way, and again, as before when she has been conscious of special joy, there came welling up in her heart a sense of her own unworthiness. Oh, that she had more grace! Oh, that she could *do* more for God, do more to bring men and women to salvation. Had *she* done what she could? Of course her pamphlet would do good; she had proclaimed the truth. But was that enough? What if women, as convinced as she herself was that they had the right to speak for Christ, did not act on their right? Was she right to have said no so swiftly when that unanimous invitation to speak to the class leaders had been given? Looking back, it seemed to her as if in the first joy of assurance about her conversion, when she was seventeen, she was more ready to obey every inner prompting than she was as a minister's wife! Of her experience in the days after Emma's birth she said,

I could not sleep at night with thinking of the state of those who die unsaved. . . . Perhaps some of you would hardly credit that I was one of the most timid and bashful disciples the Lord Jesus ever saved . . . I used to make up my mind I would, and resolve and intend, and then when the hour came, I used to fail for want of courage. . . . One day it seemed as if the Lord revealed it all to me by His Spirit. I had not a vision, but a revelation to my mind. . . . I promised Him there in the sick room, "Lord, if Thou will return unto me, as in the days of old and revisit me with those urgings of Thy Spirit which I used to have, I will obey, if I die in the attempt!"

If the Holy Spirit prompted she would obey. This was a vow.

A few months passed, and William was much in demand as a preacher beyond his own circuit. He begged Catherine to speak for some of the home meetings. But she said she felt no compelling impulse and continued to refuse. Pentecost Sunday came and a large crowd of more than a thousand had assembled. Catherine stated,

I was in the minister's pew with my eldest boy, then four years old . . . and not expecting anything particular. . . . I felt the Spirit come upon me; you alone who have felt it know what it means. It cannot be described. . . . It seemed as if a voice said to me, "Now, if you were to go and testify, you know I would bless it to your own soul as well as to the souls of the people."

124

I gasped again and I said in my soul, . . . "I cannot do it." I had forgotten my vow. It did not occur to me at all. All in a moment after I had said that to the Lord, I seemed to see the bedroom where I had lain, and to see myself . . . and then the Voice seemed to say to me, "Is this consistent with that promise?" And I almost jumped up and said, "No, Lord, it is the old thing over again, but I cannot do it.'. . . And then the devil said, "Besides, you are not prepared to speak. You will look like a fool, and have nothing to say." He made a mistake! He overdid himself for once! It was that word that settled it. I said, "Ah, this is just the point. I have never yet been willing to be a fool for Christ, now I will be one." And without stopping for another moment, I rose up in the seat, and walked up the chapel. My dear husband was just going to conclude. He stepped down from the pulpit to ask me, "What is the matter, my dear?" I said, "I want to say a word." He was taken by surprise; he could only say, "My dear wife wants to say a word," and sat down. . . . I got up—God only knows how—and if any mortal ever did hang on the arms of Omnipotence, I did. I just told the people how it came about.

It is reported the congregation was moved deeply and many wept audibly. When she finished, William jumped to his feet and announced that his wife would preach at the evening service!

That Pentecost evening in 1860, Bethesda Chapel in Gateshead was thronged with people. Catherine announced her text: "Be ye filled with the Spirit," a text she lived her entire life.

Catherine knew well the teachings of John and Charles Wesley but yearned for more. After reading the life of William Carvosso, she recorded in her journal, "Oh, what a man of faith and prayer he was! My desires after holiness have been much increased. This day I have sometimes seemed on the verge of the good land. . . yet there seems something in the way to prevent me fully entering in. . . . *I want a clean heart.*"

Catherine began to seek diligently, and many letters to her mother and others describe this seeking. To her mother she wrote, "The Lord has been dealing graciously with William for some time past. . . . He is now on full stretch for holiness. You would be amazed at the change in him. It would take me all night to detail all."

In a subsequent letter she wrote,

I had been in some degree of error with reference to the nature, or rather the manner of sanctification, regarding it rather as a great and mighty work to be wrought in me through Christ, than the simple reception of Christ as an all-sufficient Saviour, dwelling in my heart. . . . On Thursday and Friday I was totally absorbed in the subject and laid aside almost everything else and spent the chief part of the day in reading and prayer, and in trying to believe for it. On Thursday afternoon at tea-time I was well-nigh discouraged and felt my old besetment, irritability; and the devil told me I should never get it, and so I might as well give it up at once. However, I knew him of old as a liar. William and I had a blessed season and while he was saying, "Lord, we open our hearts to receive Thee," that word was spoken to my soul, "Behold I stand at the door and knock. If any man hear My voice, and open unto Me, I will come in and sup with him...." Immediately the word was given to me to confirm my faith, "Now ye are clean through the word which I have spoken unto you." And I took hold—true with a trembling hand, and not unmolested by the tempter—but I held fast the beginning of my confidence and it grew stronger. . . . I did not feel much rapturous joy, but perfect peace.

CATHERINE BOOTH

HANNAH WHITALL SMITH

CHAPTER 14

THE LORD IS ABLE
TO SAVE YOU FULLY,
NOW, IN THIS LIFE.

INTRODUCTION

Of all the people who significantly influenced the nineteenth-century Holiness Movement, Hannah Whitall Smith (1832–1911) and her husband, Robert Pearsall Smith, were "of a different kind." They were both from socially and financially prominent Philadelphia Quaker families. Wounded by the many divisions that had shattered the Friends movement, the notes of purity, power, and victorious Christian living that they heard in the rising post-Civil War Wesleyan holiness revival echoed the holiness theology of early Quakerism.

Robert found entire sanctification in a dramatic spiritual experience during the first Methodist national camp meeting at Vineland, New Jersey, in 1867.

Hannah claimed the experience soon thereafter. Both became regular lay speakers in the local union holiness revival meetings. Subsequently, no one else in the movement touched as many Christians with their writings.

In 1873, through a series of strange providences, Robert Smith found himself in the middle of the blossoming holiness/deeper-life revival in Great Britain. Breakfast meetings with some of England's leading evangelicals led to larger rallies for the "Promotion of Christian Holiness" at Oxford and in the beech groves of the luxurious Broadlands estate of William and Georgiana Cowper-Temple, attendants to Queen Victoria. The two-year public ministry that followed in England, Holland, France, Germany, and Switzerland, according to Princeton's B. B. Warfield, was one of the most dramatic bursts of evangelistic activity in Christian history. It all culminated in a meeting of more than eight thousand pastors and other leaders of the established and free churches of Great Britain and the Continent at the Brighton Convention for the Promotion of Holiness in May of 1875.

Triumph was followed by trauma. After Brighton, the Smiths went back to Philadelphia, broken and dismayed and accompanied by rumors of doctrinal deviance and moral irregularity. But the positive results of their ministry were imprinted forever on the English and European churches and their overseas missions. The revival gave birth to the Keswick Convention for the Promotion of Holiness. In Germany, Smith's ministry gave new life to the Inner City Mission Movement, revived the old pietistic cells within the established Evangelical Lutheran Church, and strengthened the American Methodist and Evangelical churches in Germany and Switzerland.

But the greatest impact on the movement and the Christian churches was made by the pen of Hannah in response to Robert's insistence that she contribute a column on the life of holiness to "The Christian's Pathway of Poet." Often driven more by the pressure of demanding deadlines than of any inspiration of the moment she wrote the columns that, in 1875, were gathered into a book. *The Christian's Secret of a Happy Life* quickly became one of the best-selling books of the nineteenth century, surpassed only by the Bible and John Bunyan's *Pilgrim's Progress*. Today, along with two other holiness classics—Oswald Chambers' *My Utmost for His Highest* and Lettie Cowman's *Streams in the Desert*—it is still one of the most widely read manuals of Christian spirituality.

—MELVIN DIETER

THE CHRISTIAN'S SECRET OF A HAPPY LIFE

CHAPTER 2: "THE SCRIPTURALNESS OF THIS LIFE"

When I approach this subject of the true Christian life, that life which is hid with Christ in God, so many thoughts struggle for utterance that I am almost speechless. Where shall I begin? What is the most important thing to say? How shall I make people read and believe? The subject is so glorious, and human words seem so powerless! But something I am impelled to say. The secret must be told. For it is one concerning that victory which overcometh the world, that promised deliverance from all our enemies, for which every child of God longs and prays, but which seems so often and so generally to elude their grasp. May God grant me so to tell it, that every believer to whom this book shall come, may have his eyes opened to see the

HANNAH WHITALL SMITH

truth as it is in Jesus, and may be enabled to enter into possession of this glorious life for himself.

For sure I am that every converted soul longs for victory and rest, and nearly every one feels instinctively, at times, that they are his birthright. Can you not remember, some of you, the shout of triumph your souls gave when you first became acquainted with the Lord Jesus, and had a glimpse of His mighty saving power? How sure you were of victory then! How easy it seemed, to be more than conquerors, through Him that loved you. Under the leadership of a Captain who had never been foiled in battle, how could you dream of defeat? And yet, to many of you, how different has been your real experience. The victories have been but few and fleeting, the defeats many and disastrous. You have not lived as you feel children of God ought to live. There has been a resting in a clear understanding of doctrinal truth, without pressing after the power and life thereof. There has been a rejoicing in the knowledge of things testified of in the Scriptures, without a living realization of the things themselves, consciously felt in the soul. Christ is believed in, talked about, and served, but He is not known as the soul's actual and very life, abiding there forever, and revealing Himself there continually in His beauty. You have found Jesus as your Saviour and your Master, and you have tried to serve Him and advance the cause of His kingdom. You have carefully studied the Holy Scriptures and have gathered much precious truth therefrom, which you have endeavored faithfully to practise.

But notwithstanding all your knowledge and all your activities in the service of the Lord, your souls are secretly starving, and you cry out again and again for that bread and water of life which you saw promised in the Scriptures to all believers. In the very depths of your hearts you know that your experience is not a Scriptural experience; that, as an old writer says, your religion is "but a talk to what the early Christians enjoyed, possessed, and lived in." And your souls have sunk within you, as day after day, and year after year, your early visions of triumph have seemed to grow more and more dim, and you have been forced to settle down to the conviction that the best you can expect from your religion is a life of alternate failure and victory; one hour sinning, and the next repenting; and beginning again, only to fail again, and again to repent.

But is this all? Had the Lord Jesus only this in His mind when He laid down His precious life to deliver you from your sore and cruel bondage to sin? Did He propose to Himself only this partial deliverance? Did He intend to leave you thus struggling along under a weary consciousness of defeat and discouragement? Did He fear that a continuous victory would dishonor Him, and bring reproach on His name? When all those declarations were made concerning His coming, and the work He was to accomplish, did they mean only this that you have experienced? Was there a hidden reserve in each promise that was meant to deprive it of its complete fulfillment? Did "delivering us out of the hands of our enemies" mean only a few of them? Did "enabling us always to triumph" mean only sometimes; or being "more than conquerors through Him that loved us" mean constant defeat and failure? No, no, a thousand times no! God is able to save unto the uttermost, and He means to do it. His promise, confirmed by His oath, was that "He would grant unto us, that we, being delivered out of the hand of our enemies, might serve Him without fear, in holiness and righteousness before Him, all the days of our life." It is a mighty work to do, but our Deliverer is able to do it. He came to destroy the works of the devil, and dare we dream for a moment that He is not able or not willing to accomplish His own purposes?

In the very outset, then, settle down on this one thing, that the Lord is able to save you fully, now, in this life, from the power and dominion of sin, and to deliver you altogether out of the hands of your enemies. If you do not think He is, search your Bible, and collect together every announcement or declaration concerning the purposes and object of His death on the cross. You will be astonished to find how full they are. Everywhere and always His work is said to be, to deliver us from our sins, from our bondage, from our defilement; and not a hint is given anywhere that this deliverance was to be only the limited and partial one with which the Church so continually tries to be satisfied.

Let me give you a few texts on this subject. When the angel of the Lord appeared unto Joseph in a dream and announced the coming birth of the Saviour, he said, "And thou shalt call His name Jesus, for He shall save His people from their sins."

When Zacharias was "filled with the Holy Ghost" at the birth of his son, and "prophesied," he declared that God had visited His people in order to fulfill the promise and the oath He had made them, which promise was, "That He would grant unto us, that we, being delivered out of the hands of our enemies, might serve Him without fear, in holiness and righteousness before Him, all the days of our life."

134   When Peter was preaching in the porch of the Temple to the wondering Jews, he said, "Unto you first, God, having raised up His Son

Jesus, sent Him to bless you in turning away every one of you from his iniquities."

When Paul was telling out to the Ephesian church the wondrous truth that Christ had loved them so much as to give Himself for them, he went on to declare that His purpose in thus doing was, "that He might sanctify and cleanse it by the washing of water by the word, that He might present it to Himself a glorious church, not having spot or wrinkle, or any such thing; but that it should be holy and without blemish."

When Paul was seeking to instruct Titus, his own son after the common faith, concerning the grace of God, he declared that the object of that grace was to teach us "that denying ungodliness and worldly lusts, we should live soberly, righteously, and godly in this present world"; and adds, as the reason of this, that Christ "gave Himself for us that He might redeem us from all iniquity, and purify us unto Himself a peculiar people, zealous of good works."

When Peter was urging upon the Christians to whom he was writing a holy and Christ-like walk, he tells them that "even here-unto were ye called because Christ also suffered for us, leaving us an example that ye should follow His steps: who did no sin, neither was guile found in His mouth"; and adds, "who His own self bare our sins in His own body on the tree, that we, being dead to sins, should live unto righteousness; by whose stripes ye were healed."

When Paul was contrasting in the Ephesians the walk suitable for a Christian, with the walk of an unbeliever, he sets before them the truth in Jesus as being this, "that ye put off concerning the former 135 conversation the old man, which is corrupt according to the deceitful lusts; and be renewed in the spirit of your mind; and that ye put on the new man, which after God is created in righteousness and true holiness."

And when, in Romans 6, he was answering forever the question as to continuing in sin, and showing how utterly foreign it was to the whole spirit and aim of the salvation of Jesus, he brings up the fact of our judicial death and resurrection with Christ as an unanswerable argument for our practical deliverance from it, and says, "God forbid. How shall we, that are dead to sin, live any longer therein? Know ye not that so many of us as were baptized into Jesus Christ were baptized into His death? Therefore we are buried with Him by baptism into death; that like as Christ was raised up from the dead by the glory of the Father, even so we also should walk in newness of life." And adds, "Knowing this, that our old man is crucified with Him, that the body of sin might be destroyed, that henceforth we should not serve sin."

Dear Christians, will you receive the testimony of Scripture on this matter? The same questions that troubled the Church in Paul's day are troubling it now: first, "Shall we continue in sin that grace may abound?" And second, "Do we then make void the law through faith?" Shall not our answer to these be Paul's emphatic "God forbid"; and his triumphant assertions that instead of making it void "we establish the law"; and that "what the law could not do, in that it was weak through the flesh, God sending His own Son in the likeness of sinful flesh, and for sin, condemned sin in the flesh: that the righteousness of the law might be fulfilled in us who walk not after the flesh, but after the Spirit"?

136   Can we suppose for a moment that the holy God, who hates sin in the sinner, is willing to tolerate it in the Christian, and that He has

even arranged the plan of salvation in such a way as to make it impossible for those who are saved from the guilt of sin to find deliverance from its power? . . .

Surely, then, we will not dare to think that it is impossible for the creature whom God has made, to accomplish the declared object for which he was created. Especially when the Scriptures are so full of the assertions that Christ has made it possible.

HANNAH WHITALL SMITH

THOMAS **COOK**

CHAPTER 15

INTRODUCTION

Thomas Cook (1859–1913), though little known in the United States, was a famous evangelist in Great Britain around the turn of the twentieth century. Born in Middlesborough, Yorkshire, England, on August 20, 1859, he was heavily influenced as a child by the godly Christian witness of his mother. When Cook came to know the Lord in 1875, his first stop afterward was his mother's sickbed, saying, "Mother, I have given myself to Jesus tonight."

Thomas Cook studied for the ordained ministry in the Wesleyan Methodist Connection (England). He became a local preacher in 1878, but was turned down for ordination by the conference. However, he was such an effective lay evangelist that they changed their minds and ordained him in 1882. Thousands of people in that generation came to know Christ as Savior through his ministry.

Thomas Cook went on to serve as the first principal of Cliff College, a training center for Wesleyan Methodist ministers in England. He is most famous for writing the classic work, *New Testament Holiness*, a selection of which is featured here.

In Chapter 5, "The New Birth and Entire Sanctification," Dr. Cook examines the relationship of regeneration to entire sanctification. Often in the teaching of holiness, the first work of grace, regeneration, has been minimized to make room for a definite second work of grace. This is unfortunate, indeed, for as Dr. Cook indicates, "regeneration is holiness begun."

He also clearly emphasizes that when a person is converted he is already sanctified in that, "he is set apart for God; a new and heavenly life is breathed into him by the Holy Spirit; he enjoys victory over the world and sin." This is called "initial sanctification." He points out that while "the dominion of sin is broken," regeneration does not "free the soul from depravity." The regenerate believer is saved from sins committed but the disposition itself remains. The inward corruption, although now under the control of a "stronger gracious power," still makes resistance, indicating its presence and the need to be entirely sanctified. Dr. Cook's comparison of the two makes an important contribution to the understanding of the holiness message.

Dr. Cook lays bare what we could describe as the traditional view of entire sanctification. That is, he describes the sin nature as a "thing" or an "entity" that can and must be "eradicated." It must be said that there are holiness theologians who would argue that naming the sinful nature as a "thing to be eradicated" is not the best way to describe original or inherited sin. They would view the sin nature more as a disease from which one must be cleansed rather than an abscessed tooth that must be removed. However, both the world and the Church are served by the declaration of a grace that meets the totality of human need for redemp-

140

tion in the here and now. That is the triumph of grace in Dr. Cook's teaching, and that is the triumph of grace offered to every believer.

—EARLE WILSON

NEW TESTAMENT HOLINESS

CHAPTER 5: "THE NEW BIRTH AND ENTIRE SANCTIFICATION"

Divine forgiveness and the new birth are ever coexistent and inseparable. No man receives the new name of a child of God without at the same time receiving a new nature. He becomes there and then a partaker of the Divine holiness. Condemnation is removed, the culprit is forgiven, and as invariably as day follows night, a sublime change is wrought by the Holy Spirit, creating within the soul a new spiritual life, a life of loyalty and love.

The Scriptures describe this work of the Holy Spirit as a new creation, a being "born again," "born of the Spirit"; a passing "from death unto life," "quickened with Christ," and by many like expressions all indicating newness and sanctity. It is such a renewal of the soul as turns preponderating tendencies toward God; the love of sin is destroyed, the power of sin is broken, and a desire and relish for holiness is begotten.

In a measure and to a certain extent the Christian is sanctified when he is regenerated. He is set apart for God. He is made a new creature in Christ Jesus. A new and heavenly life is breathed into him by the Holy Spirit. He is translated out of darkness into marvelous light. The

141

dominion of sin is broken. The love of God is shed abroad in his heart, which is the incentive to obedience, and the germ of holiness. His desires, tastes, impulses, aims, and aspirations are all changed. He no longer "lives unto himself," "his life is hid with Christ in God." He has victory over the world and sin, enjoys inward peace, walks before God in newness of life, and loving God, keeps His commandments.

Regeneration is holiness begun. Whatever is of the essence of holiness is found in germ in all who are children of God. But though all the elements of holiness are imparted, the work of inward renewal is only begun, not finished, by regeneration. On this point there is harmony of faith among all the Churches. They hold that regeneration does not free the soul from depravity. It introduces a power which checks the outbreaking of depravity into actual sin, but inward corruption remains, manifesting itself in a bias toward evil, in inclinations to sin, in a proneness to depart from God, "a bent to sinning." Says Bishop Foster: "Sin committed, and depravity felt, are very different: the one is an action, the other a state of the affections. The regenerate believer is saved from the one, and he has grace to enable him to have victory over the other; but the disposition itself to some extent remains, under the control of a stronger gracious power implanted, but still making resistance, and indicating actual presence, and needing to be entirely sanctified."

It is by no means uncommon for persons to imagine at the time of forgiveness that depravity is completely destroyed. The change is so great, even as "from death unto life," that the work of moral renovation seems perfect. The love and gladness of the newborn soul is so overflowing, as for a time to create the impression that the heart is entirely cleansed. "How easily do they draw the inference, I feel no sin, therefore I have none; it does not stir, therefore it does not exist;

it has no motion, therefore it has no being. But it is seldom long before they are undeceived, finding sin was only suspended, not destroyed." When this occurs the new convert is often surprised and alarmed, and sometimes deems his conversion a failure, not knowing the Scriptures or the two-fold nature of sin.

In regeneration sin is subdued and conquered, but it is not destroyed. The fortress of Mansoul has been won for its legitimate Lord, but within its garrison some traitors lurk, maimed and bleeding, but not dead. The disease is modified, but it is not eradicated. The bitter and baneful thing is nipped in the bud, some of the branches are lopped off, but the root is not removed. Depravity is suspended, held in check, repressed; but it is not fully expelled from the soul. It does not reign, but it exists. Tendencies to sin are controlled, but they are not extirpated. There is still a warfare within, a sort of duality, in which flesh and spirit antagonize each other. It is a state of mixedness, in which Christians in a degree, according to the measure of their faith, are spiritual, yet in a degree they are carnal. We would not for a moment minify the great and glorious work of conversion, but all experience testifies that an "infection of nature does remain, warring against the Spirit even in those who are regenerate." The result often is that from the germ-sins in the heart spring actual sins in the life.

Regeneration is the beginning of purification. Entire sanctification is the finishing of that work. Entire sanctification removes from the soul all the elements that antagonize the elements of holiness planted in regeneration. It is an elimination, as dross is separated from the gold by fire. It is an eradication, the removal of all roots of bitterness, the seeds of sin's disease. It is a crucifixion, the putting to death of the 143 body or the life of sin. It is such a complete renewal of the heart that

THOMAS COOK

sin has no longer any place within, its last remains are scattered, the war within the citadel ceases and God reigns without a rival.

There are those who teach that entire sanctification consists in the power of the Holy Spirit repressing inbred sin, holding in check our sinful proclivities, choking down the old man instead of putting him to death. When the apostle speaks of the body of sin being destroyed (Rom. 6:6) they tone down the meaning of the word destroyed, and explain it as meaning to render inert or inoperative; but Dr. Steele with his critical research points out the strength of the word by comparing it with the following texts where the same word is rendered "abolish," "consume," or "destroy": 2 Corinthians 3:13; Ephesians 2:15; 2 Timothy 1:10; 1 Corinthians 6:13; 1 Corinthians 15:26; 2 Thessalonians 2:8; Hebrews 2:14. We have no fear of the result of a careful investigation of these texts by unprejudiced and candid minds.

The same writer also calls attention to the fact, that while the Greek language abounds in words signifying repression, a half-score of which occur in the New Testament, and are translated by to bind, bruise, cast down, bring into bondage, repress, hinder, restrain, subdue, take by the throat, yet none of these is ever used of inbred sin, but such verbs as signify to cleanse, to purify, to mortify or kill, to crucify, and to destroy. "We have diligently sought," he says, "in both the Old Testament and the New, for exhortations to seek the repression of sin. The uniform command is to put away sin, to purify the heart, to purge out the old leaven, to seek to be sanctified throughout spirit, soul and body. Repressive power is nowhere ascribed to the blood of Christ, but rather purifying efficacy. Now if these verbs, which signify to cleanse, wash, crucify, mortify, or make dead, and to destroy, are all used in a metaphorical sense, it is evident that the literal truth signified is some-

144

thing far stronger than repression. It is eradication, extinction of being, destruction." Here is surely sufficient warrant for the prayer:

Every deed and thought unruly
Do to death; for He has died.

This teaching is confirmed also by the prayer, already referred to, which St. Paul offered for the Thessalonians, "And the very God of peace sanctify you wholly." The word "sanctify" has two principal meanings: (1) to dedicate, or set apart, things or persons to sacred purposes; (2) to cleanse or purify. In the prayer before us the word is used in the latter sense, and to denote the thoroughness and pervasive nature of the purification prayed for, the apostle uses a strong word which is found nowhere else in the New Testament. Commentators agree that the word translated "wholly" is one of the strongest words that could possibly be used to express complete deliverance from spiritual pollution. Dr. Mahan says it is compounded of two words, one meaning all, the other perfection. Dr. Adam Clarke says the original word signifies precisely the same as our English phrase "to all intents and purposes." Luther translates it "through and through." In the Vulgate it is rendered "in your collective powers and parts." Mr. Wesley says it means every part of you perfectly. If full deliverance from sin is not taught in this prayer, it is not within the power of human language to teach it. Thrice welcome the assurance that follows the prayer: "Faithful is He that calleth you, who also will do it."

Do any ask what is the exact difference between regeneration and entire sanctification? It is this: the one has remaining impurity; the other has none. We do not say that entire sanctification embraces nothing more than complete cleansing from sin—it does. It is the full gracious endowment of perfect love, and much else, but with the positive aspects of holiness we will deal later. It is sufficient in this chapter to set forth the fact that entire sanctification completes the work of purification and renovation begun in regeneration.

SAMUEL LOGAN
BRENGLE

CHAPTER 16

FOLLOWING GOD
MEANS THAT WE MUST
BE HOLY HERE,
AND NOW.

INTRODUCTION

Samuel Logan Brengle (1860–1936) was born in Fredricksburg, Indiana, in June of 1860. He was converted around the age of twelve at a revival meeting held in Olney, Illinois, where his family had relocated. Brengle completed his A.B. at Depauw University in 1883 (then known as Indiana Asbury University), where he distinguished himself as an orator.

Having been raised in the Methodist Episcopal Church, his call to the ministry led him for a short time to serve as a Methodist circuit-riding preacher. He pressed on in 1885 for theological education by enrolling at Boston Theological Seminary, where he came under the influence of the renowned holiness scholar Professor Daniel Steele. That very year, Brengle was exposed to the winsome and rigorous persuasion of Steele's advocacy of entire sanctification, and Brengle came personally to experience holiness of heart, "the Blessing." This experience would radiate through his entire life and ministry.

Later that same year (1885), Brengle came across some of the writings of Catherine Booth, and then was able to hear General Booth himself (of Salvation Army fame) preaching in the Tremont Temple Church hall. Brengle was so impressed by the holiness message of the Salvation Army movement that he plunged deeply into connection with it. He married one of its preachers (Elizabeth Swift) and voyaged to England to meet with General Booth and enter into officer training.

Brengle returned to the United States for assignment in various corps, including one in Boston. It was there that he sustained a serious head injury while he was preaching. A drunken man in an act of revenge hurled a brick that struck Brengle, requiring an extensive period (about a year and a half) of rest and recuperation. But in the mystery of divine providence, this very period of time that might have sidelined Brengle from the work of the ministry became the golden span that launched his powerful writing career. He submitted a series of articles to the Salvation Army's periodical, *The War Cry*, and later published collections of these articles in book form as *Helps to Holiness*, and later, *The Soul-Winner's Secret*. Other noteworthy works include *Heart Talks on Holiness*, *The Way of Holiness*, and *When the Holy Ghost Is Come*.

Brengle's stature grew in the Salvation Army, and he became the first American officer to become a commissioner. His wisdom guided the Army through several severe tests and growing pains, especially those involving the shift of the movement out from under the control of the Booth family. In terms of Brengle's holiness legacy, it appears 150 that he managed to set forth the holiness message in a down-to-earth style often punctuated with real-life illustrations. He urged for the blessing to be received "now," but did not preach a "name it, claim it" approach. He exhorted all seekers and professors of holiness to avoid the extremes of wild, irrational emotionalism on the one hand, and cold, hard formalism or rationalism on the other. He also proved in his writing and in his worldwide preaching campaigns that holiness not only can be wedded to evangelism, but naturally compels it by the fires of love.

—JOSEPH DONGELL

THE WAY OF HOLINESS

CHAPTER IV: "WHEN CAN WE BE MADE HOLY?"

Before we can be holy, this "old man" must be put off, this evil within must die, this seed of all sin must be destroyed, and this is something that can and does take place just as soon after conversion as we see the need and the possibility of its being done, and come to Jesus with all our heart, and with perfect faith to have it done.

Some people say that we cannot get rid of this evil nature until we die; but we must stick to the Bible and believe what that book says. And the Bible certainly teaches that we can be made holy in this life. The Bible says, "Be ye holy"; and that means now, not after death. If a man says to his boy, "Be honest, be truthful," he means, Be honest and truthful now, for *this* world, not in Heaven only. And so God 151 means that we must be holy here, and now.

SAMUEL LOGAN BRENGLE

Again the Bible says, "Put off . . . the old man, which is corrupt . . . and put on the new man, which after God is created in righteousness and true holiness" (Eph. 4:22–24). We are told to "put off all these; anger, wrath, malice, blasphemy, filthy communication out of your mouth." And we are told to "be filled with the Spirit." All this is to take place now.

I shall never forget how one Sunday afternoon, after hearing of the possibility and blessedness of a pure heart, a beautiful girl of sixteen walked straight up to the platform, fell on her knees, and lifting her face to Heaven with tears, told the Lord how she wanted a clean heart filled with the Holy Spirit just then. She saw that she need not wait, but that now was the accepted time. And oh! How God blessed her! Soon the smiles were chasing away the tears, and the joy of Heaven was shining on her face. Years after, I found her on the platform, a Lieutenant, with her face still shining, and her heart still cleansed.

And so, my dear young Comrade, this priceless blessing may be yours. Jesus has died to purchase this uttermost salvation, and it is your Heavenly Father's will for you, just now. Have faith in God, give yourself utterly to Him, even now, and begin to seek the blessing with a determination never to stop seeking until it is yours, and you shall not be long without it. Praise the Lord!

CHAPTER VI: "HOLINESS AND THE SANCTIFICATION OF THE BODY"

Athletes, football and cricket players, and prize-fighters when in training are exceedingly careful about their health. They select their food with care and eat nothing that would disagree with them, omitting heavy suppers; they abstain from strong drink and tobacco; they bathe their bodies daily; they go to bed and get up at regular hours;

152

they sleep with open windows, and, of course, they have plenty of fresh air and systematic exercise. This they do for months, and sometimes for years, simply that they may beat some other fellows in contests of strength and skill. Now they do it, says Paul, "to obtain a corruptible crown, but we an incorruptible." And then he adds, "I keep under my body, and bring it into subjection: lest that by any means, when I have preached to others, I myself should be a castaway" (1 Cor. 9:25–27).

I know a man who noticed that when he ate too much he became irritable, and was subject to various temptations from which a careful diet freed him. He had to control his appetite in order to keep a clean heart.

Young people are likely to squander their health in all sorts of useless and careless ways, and are tempted to laugh and sneer at their elders when they lift a warning voice. But they will some day find that advance in holiness, progress toward Heaven, and happiness and usefulness are more dependent on the right care of the body than they supposed.

"Beloved, I wish above all things that thou mayest prosper and be in good health even as thy soul prospereth" (3 John 2).

CHAPTER VIII: "HOLINESS AND HUMILITY"

Those who oppose holiness often say that we who profess it are proud, and that the doctrine tends to spiritual pride. But the truth is that holiness goes down to the root of all pride and digs it up utterly. A holy man is one who has found himself out, and pronounced judgment against himself, and come to Jesus to be made every whit whole. And so long as he keeps the blessing, he is deeply humble.

This is a certain effect of entire sanctification. The sinful heart apologizes for itself, excuses inbred sin, favors it, argues for it. A man who still has the carnal mind says, "I think one ought to have a little pride. I would not give a snap of my finger for a man who had not some temper. A man who will not stand up for his rights is weak." And so he excuses, and argues in favor of, the sin in his own heart.

Not so the man who is holy. He remembers his former pride, and loathes himself for it, and longs and prays to sink deeper and deeper into the infinite ocean of his Savior's humility, until every trace and stain of pride are forever washed away. He remembers his hasty temper, and hates it, and cries day and night for the perfect meekness of the Lamb of God, who, like a sheep before her shearers, "opened not His mouth," while His enemies worked their fiendish will; and, so far from smiting back, would not even talk back, but prayed, "Father, forgive them."

[The true seeker] sees the beauty of God's holiness, and loves it. He sees the full extent of his former corruption, and acknowledges and loathes it. Before, he thought man had some natural goodness, but now he knows and confesses that "the whole head is sick, and the whole heart faint. From the sole of the foot even unto the head there is no soundness in it; but wounds, and bruises, and putrifying sores" (Isaiah 1:5–6).

He sees his own evil ways. At one time he thought that there was not one holy man on earth, for he could see a mote in every man's eye; but now he discovers that there are many holy men, and the mote which he was sure he saw in his neighbor's eye, he now finds to have been the shadow of the beam that was in his own eye.

An earnest, sanctified man once said to me, "There are certain sins I once thought it was morally impossible for me to commit, but the Holy Spirit has shown me the awful deceitfulness of my heart, and I now see that before He cleansed me there were in me the seeds of all iniquity, and there is no sin I might not have committed, and no depth of moral degradation to which I might not have sunk, but for the restraining grace of God."

One who has thus seen the plague of his own heart may be cleansed in the precious Blood, and may have a holy heart, but he will never say to another, "Stand thou there, for I am holier than thou"; but, remembering his own former condition, he will point him to the Lamb of God, which taketh away the sins of the world.

CHAPTER X: "HOLINESS AND ZEAL FOR SOULS"

"Follow me, and I will make you fishers of men," said Jesus to Peter and Andrew; and now as then when Jesus saves a soul, that soul wants to catch men, wants to see others saved. Holiness increases this desire, and makes it burn with a quenchless flame.

The zeal of other people blazes up, burns low, and often dies out, but the zeal of a man with a clean heart, full of the Holy Ghost, increases year by year. Others run away from the prayer meeting, but he holds on. Others do not grieve if souls are not saved, or die. Others are zealous for "big goes," tea parties, ice-cream suppers, and musical festivals, but nothing pleases him so much as a prayer-meeting where souls are crying to God for pardon and cleansing, and others are shouting for joy.

And this zeal for the salvation and sanctification of men leads him 155 to do something to reach them. He lets his light shine. He speaks to people not only from the platform and the pulpit at long range, but he buttonholes them, and speaks to them wherever he finds them. Holiness makes it easy for him to do this. He loves to do it. He finds that, as he follows the Spirit, the Lord fills his mouth with truth, and gives him something to say.

E. STANLEY JONES

CHAPTER 17

MANY PHILOSOPHERS SPECULATE
ON HOW EVIL ENTERED THE WORLD—
JESUS PRESENTS HIMSELF AS
THE WAY BY WHICH IT SHALL LEAVE

INTRODUCTION

Eli Stanley Jones (1884–1973) was widely recognized as one of the greatest missionaries of the twentieth century. His great love for Jesus gave birth to a great love for the entire world. This fire that set his heart ablaze chased him to the ends of the earth with a message of freedom, grace, and restoration.

E. Stanley Jones was raised in Baltimore, Maryland. In 1901, at the age of seventeen, he experienced conversion under the ministry of an evangelist named Robert J. Bateman. Under Bateman's preaching, the Holy Spirit gripped young Stanley's heart. In his autobiography, *A Song of Ascents*, he would later describe the experience: "I had scarcely bent my knees when Heaven broke into my spirit. I was enveloped by assurance, by acceptance, by reconciliation . . . I had Him—Jesus—and He had me . . . As I rose from my knees, I felt I wanted to put my arms around the world to share this with everybody . . . This was a seed moment. The whole of my future was packed into it."

Feeling a call to become a preacher himself, Stanley enrolled in Asbury College in the tiny town of Wilmore, Kentucky. Here he was filled and formed by the Holy Spirit. Following graduation, he was offered a position as a missionary to India. In a pivotal session of intense prayer for God's direction, he felt the voice of the Lord say, "It's India." Rising up, Jones set his face, and his heart, toward the East.

The ministry and Christian influence of E. Stanley Jones had a dynamic impact across the continent. He gave himself to the work of understanding the context in which he served, falling in love with the beautiful people and rich heritage of India. It was within this context, and to this culture, that he sought to present the message and person of Jesus Christ. His classic work, *The Christ of the Indian Road*, revolutionized the theory and method of missions outside of the West, calling for a preaching of Jesus that removed the restraints of Western cultural structures.

His service to Christ placed him at the crossroads of history. He worked with President Franklin D. Roosevelt, hoping to prevent war with Japan. They sat together on December 3, 1941, days before the attack on Pearl Harbor. He became personal friends with Mahatma Gandhi, the leader of India's independence movement. E. Stanley Jones' clear and consistent witness of Christ only strengthened Gandhi's deep admiration for Jesus. As a result of their friendship, Jones was moved to write Gandhi's biography. Years later, another leader of a nonviolent freedom movement thanked him for it. After reading this account of Gandhi's unswerving commitment to peace, this man felt convinced that the same could work for the American Civil Rights Movement. His name was Dr. Martin Luther King, Jr. The world recognized Stanley's commitment to reconciliation, and he was nominated for the Nobel Peace Prize in 1962 and received the Gandhi Peace Award in 1963.

He worked for spiritual and social transformation, not because he was an activist, but because he was a Christian. The natural outgrowth of holiness theology is a love for God that leads to a love for others. This young boy who had experienced reconciliation at a revival altar spent seventy years of his life carrying the same hope to the ends of the world, and the far frontiers of the Kingdom.

—MATT LEROY

THE CHRIST OF THE INDIAN ROAD

THE MOTIVE AND THE END

If the end and motive of Christianity, and therefore of Christian missions, is to produce Christlike character, I have no apology for being a Christian missionary, for I know nothing higher for God or man than to be Christlike.

I know nothing higher for God. If God in character is like Jesus, He is a good God and trustable. The present-day doubt is not concerning Christ, but concerning God. Men wonder if there can be a good God back of things when they see earthquakes wipe out the innocent and the guilty alike and innocent little children suffer under nameless diseases that they did not bring on themselves. But the distracted and doubting mind turns with relief toward Jesus and says, "If God is like that, He is all right." As Christians we affirm that He is—that He is 161 Christlike in character, and we say it without qualification and without

E. STANLEY JONES

the slightest stammering of the tongue. We believe that "God is Jesus everywhere" and Jesus is God here—the human life of God.

If God thinks in terms of little children as Jesus did, cares for the leper, the outcast, and the blind, and if His heart is like that gentle heart that broke upon the cross, then He can have my heart without reservation and without question.

If the finest spirits of the human race should sit down and think out the kind of a God they would like to see in the universe, his moral and spiritual likeness would gradually form like unto the Son of Man. The greatest news that has ever been broken to the human race is the news that God is like Christ.

Further, I know nothing higher for man than to be Christlike. The highest adjective descriptive of character in any language is the adjective "Christlike." No higher compliment can be paid to human nature than to be called Christlike.

We thoughtfully throw down this ideal before the philosophers of the world, the statesmen, the moralists, the reformers, the religious thinkers, and we say to them: "Brother men, this is what we are trying to produce. We think it is worthwhile to produce Christlike character. Do you know anything finer and better? Do you know of any nobler goal? Is there any pattern which you have conceived that surpasses this in being just what life ought to be? If so, show us, and we will, before God, we will leave this and seek the other." I believe that the lips of the world are dumb and silent before the question of finding anything better. In the realm of character, Jesus has the field.

Now the cross never knows defeat, for it itself is Defeat, and you cannot defeat Defeat. You cannot break Brokenness. It starts with defeat and accepts that as a way of life. But in that very attitude it

162

finds its victory. It never knows when it is defeated, for it turns every impediment into an instrument, and every difficulty into a door, every cross into a means of redemption. So, I concluded, any people that would put the cross at the center of its thought and life would never know when it is defeated. It would have a quenchless hope that Easter morning lies just behind every Calvary.

We are there because Christlike character is the highest that we know, because He gives men a free, full life, and most important of all, He gives them God. And we do not know of anyone else who does do these things except Christ. But He does.

And to the heart that has learned to love Him it is irresistible to think of Him hungry, thirsty, sick, in prison, naked, a stranger in the throbbing needs of our brother men.

We take them Christ—we go to Him. He is the motive and the end.

THE SUPREMACY OF JESUS

Many who have looked for the Kingdom to come only by observation so that they could say "Lo, here," and "Lo, there," have been disappointed to find it come so slowly, but the more discerning have suddenly awakened to find that the Kingdom was in the midst of them and all around them. Christianity is actually breaking out beyond the borders of the Christian Church and is being seen in the most unexpected places. If those who have not the spirit of Jesus are none of His, no matter what outward symbols they possess, then conversely those who have the spirit of Jesus are His, no matter what outward symbols they may lack. In a spiritual movement like that of Jesus it is difficult and impossible to mark its frontiers. Statistics and classifications lose their meaning and are impotent to tell who are in and who are out. Jesus told us it would be so.

163

E. STANLEY JONES

India is the land of mysticism. You feel it in the very air. Jesus was the supreme mystic. The Unseen was real to Him. He spent all night in prayer and communion with the Father. He lived in God and God lived in Him. When He said, " I and the Father are one," you feel it is so.

Jesus the mystic appeals to India, the land of mysticism. But Jesus the mystic was amazingly concrete and practical. Into an atmosphere filled with speculation and wordy disputation where "men are often drunk with the wine of their own wordiness" He brings the refreshing sense of practical reality. He taught, but He did not speculate. Even His words had a concrete feeling about them. They fell upon the soul with the authority of certainty.

He did not speculate on why temptation should be in this world— He met it, and after forty days' struggle with it in the wilderness, He conquered, and "returned in the power of the Spirit to Galilee."

We do not find Him discoursing on the necessity of letting one's light shine at home among kinsmen and friends—He announced His program of uplift and healing at Nazareth, His own home, and those who heard "wondered at the words of grace which proceeded from his mouth."

As He came among men He did not try to prove the existence of God—He brought Him. He lived in God, and men looking upon His face could not find within themselves to doubt God.

He did not argue, as Socrates, the immortality of the soul—He raised the dead.

He did not argue that God answers prayer—He prayed, sometimes all night, and in the morning "the power of the Lord was present to heal."

164 He did not paint in glowing colors the beauties of friendship and the need for human sympathy—He wept at the grave of His friend.

He did not argue the worth of womanhood and the necessity for giving them equal rights—He treated them with infinite respect, gave them His most sublime teaching, and when He arose from the dead He appeared first to a woman.

He did not discourse on the equal worth of personality—He went to the poor and the outcast and ate with them.

He did not prove how pain and sorrow in the universe could be compatible with the love of God—He took on himself at the cross everything that spoke against the love of God, and through that pain and tragedy and sin showed the very love of God.

He did not discourse on how the weakest human material can be transformed and made to contribute to the welfare of the world—He called to Him a set of weak men, as the Galilean fishermen, transformed them and sent them out to begin the mightiest movement for uplift and redemption the world has ever seen.

He did not merely tell us that death need have no terror for us—He rose from the dead, and lo, now the tomb glows with light.

Many teachers of the world have tried to explain everything—they changed little or nothing. Jesus explained little and changed everything.

Many teachers have tried to diagnose the disease of humanity—Jesus cures it.

Many teachers have told us why the patient is suffering and that he should bear it with fortitude—Jesus tells him to take up his bed and walk.

Many philosophers speculate on how evil entered the world—Jesus presents himself as the way by which it shall leave.

He didn't go into long discussions about the way to God and the possibility of finding Him—He quietly said to men, "I am the Way." 165

E. STANLEY JONES

ROY S. NICHOLSON

CHAPTER 18

THE SUPREME MOTIVE
FOR HOLINESS
IS GOD HIMSELF.

INTRODUCTION

In our day of unashamed moral compromise within the Church and rampant evil embraced by our North American culture, the prophetic voice of Dr. Roy S. Nicholson (1903–1993) rings clear with the biblical message of holiness. The following article is an inviting taste of his life and writings. During his generation of the early twentieth century, he was perhaps the most influential voice for holiness across The Wesleyan Methodist Church, which he served as General Conference president from 1947–1959. He was an articulate speaker, prolific writer, capable leader, and effective professor. However, his greatest impact and legacy rests upon the sterling example of his life and the commendation this gave to his central message from God's Holy Word: "We are to be holy because God is holy."

Those who knew Dr. Nicholson personally were keenly aware of his gentle, Christlike spirit, his walk of humility before God, his loving concern for others, and his passion to see everyone transformed by the power of the Holy Spirit. He preached and taught with confidence in God's will and power to radically alter the moral nature of man, resulting in a will that obeys God without conscious reservation and a heart that has been set ablaze with the love of God. He was a powerful spokesman for holiness.

The message Dr. Nicholson lived and preached was quintessentially a biblical message. He preached the Word of God and did not hesitate to call the Church to the higher ground of holiness for both character and conduct. He preached the truth with persuasive clarity and with equally compelling love. In knowing Dr. Nicholson, you were drawn to know God; both drew you to be holy.

The following article by Dr. Nicholson, taken from a lecture series he gave at Eastern Pilgrim College in Allentown, Pennsylvania, in 1962, graciously opens up the heart of holiness—its supreme motive found in the very nature of God. This holy God is our life, and through that life, we can be holy because he is holy. The nature of God is to hate sin, and by his goodness, wisdom, and power he calls his people everywhere to respond in faith to the promises and purposes of God the Father, Son, and Holy Spirit—and be transformed into his holy likeness. From the core of our being to every conduct and conversation of life, God calls us to be holy. We can and must be, for such is the life that is well pleasing to God.

For a new generation, this is a radical message of hope. God has told us clearly that he has the power to make holy the character of the human heart; it is his explicit will to do so. The horrors of the last century have confirmed the depth of humanity's depravity, and the wickedness that abounds in our day cries out for the people of God to be holy. Will God find men and women today who will walk with him in the blazing fire and purity of holiness? May there be a revival of Christlike holiness that rises above our cultural Christianity and declares to the world, "The one who has called us to be holy is faithful, and he will do it." The life and writings of Dr. Nicholson can surely stoke that fire.

—DAVID MEDDERS

THE SUPREME MOTIVE FOR HOLINESS

The Scriptural basis for this message is found in 1 Peter 1:15 and 16: "But as he which hath called you is holy, so be ye holy in all manner of conversation; Because it is written, 'Be ye holy, for I am holy.'" These verses give us the model for holiness and the motive for holiness. This is a command that is made blessed by reason of the motive that enforces it. As we develop this study, two truths ought to be kept in mind: (1) Because of God's nature and His relationship to man as Creator and Father, it is right that man should bear His character; (2) because of man's nature, and his relationship to God, created in the image of God, and created "redeemable," it is possible for him to partake in the character (or holiness) of God. "Holiness is God's Choice for the moral condition of man."

THE HOLINESS OF WHICH WE SPEAK

There are many and varied terms which have been used to define and describe this glorious truth of the doctrine, the experience and the

ROY S. NICHOLSON

life of holiness. Some are Biblical and some are extra-Biblical. They are so numerous and so well-known that they shall not be enumerated here. Suffice it to say that the holiness of which we speak is "moral likeness to God." It is that principle which characterizes God. It is God's standard for man's moral character. It is that character which is so indispensable to man's well-being that he cannot be happy without it.

Dr. Paul S. Rees has defined holiness as "the moral quality of the character of those who, through the indwelling of the Holy Spirit, share Christ's nature and consent to be ruled by it."

The New Testament does not hesitate to apply the same terms to man's perfection or holiness, as are applied to God. Man is bidden to be "holy as He is holy." Man is holy when he is brought by grace into "perfect moral sonship and obedience" to God, a relationship to God "by which the Divine righteousness may be honored and conserved."

New Testament holiness is merely sinlessness; that is, purity and abstention from known sin, "it implies the constant activity and positive exercise of all goodness in the realm of daily life." This holiness is not only the deliverance of the soul from the guilt of sin but from the power and presence of sin. This results from the believer's union with, and constant dwelling in Him, "who is the negation of all sin, and its destroyer, and who came not only to impute but also to impart righteousness, even as he is righteous."

To receive this holiness there must be harmony of will with the will of God, a perfect self-devotion to God, complete death to self, and "absolute submission" to God. Only when these conditions are met can man be a partaker of the Divine Nature and be holy "as he who hath called you is holy."

As we think of the goal for our spiritual life, it will be well to keep in mind George Gritter's formula as outlined in *The Quest for Holiness*: "The Holy Spirit in guiding us to spiritual maturity always has these four things in mind: (1) fuller enjoyment of God; (2) more devout worship of God; (3) more efficient service of God; (4) preparation for eternity with God." From the above it is apparent that the goal is not to be found in man but in God.

The motive is there: The will of God is that His children receive a new nature or principle of life, which works from the heart to the outward life through a radical transformation or renewal of the mind (Romans 12:2; 1 Peter 4:1). That produces a godly character which reveals God's likeness by showing one to be God's child. By this transformation he is able to think God's thoughts and to do God's will without conscious reservation.

This experience of holiness, wrought in the believer by the Holy Spirit, has only one great aim—to glorify Christ (John 16:14). When He (the Holy Spirit) comes to dwell in the heart in all the fullness of His power as the Sanctifier, it is for that one purpose—to glorify Jesus Christ. Holiness is not an end in itself: God says to us "Be ye holy" because He knows that only holiness can witness to His glory.

The supreme motive for holiness is God Himself. His nature is the supreme and all-sufficient motive. Holiness is necessary because any sin is utterly offensive to God; whether it be in the inner nature or in the outward conduct of man.

The whole tenor of Scripture clearly reveals that God from His holiness hates sin. God from His goodness has moved to redeem man from all sin. God in His wisdom understands how salvation from sin 171 may be accomplished. God by His power is able to produce in man that moral character He most desires. Salvation from sin is both possible to God and consistent with His eternal purpose, love and government. Therefore, it is possible for man, in this life.

Those propositions are supported by the nature of God, the will of God, the calls of God, the commands of God, the eternal purpose of God, the power of God, the prayers of Christ, and the unfailing promises of God.

Our own hearts take up the theme, and every throb enforces it, but many smother the voice and will not hearken. But when man has made his greatest show of wisdom and exhibited his greatest display of logic in objecting to holiness of heart as a present, personal experience of cleansing from all sin as a fitness for heaven, the command of the Lord God Almighty will echo down the corridors of Eternity: "Ye shall be holy, for I am holy."

That is the supreme motive for holiness!

DENNIS F. KINLAW

CHAPTER 19

JESUS CHANGED THE PATTERN
OF PERSONAL PRIORITIES WHEN
HE BECAME THE SHEPHERD
WHO SACRIFICED HIMSELF
FOR HIS SHEEP.

INTRODUCTION

Whenever I find myself passing through his town, I make it a point to stop and see Dr. Dennis Kinlaw (1922–). I pull up a chair across from this wise man and listen—and learn. Seminary professor, college president, beloved author, and tireless evangelist, Dr. Kinlaw has served the Kingdom in a number of roles. His enduring legacy will be his gift and passion to make plain the gospel of Jesus Christ. He is included in this book as a voice from our own time, a modern expression of the holiness message.

He is a man known for his knowledge of and love affair with the Word of God. Kinlaw almost always begins his sermons with the Text. He presumes it is already relevant and needs only to be explained. In this he is different from some holiness writers of the past, who depended on rhetoric more than Text, and he is different from many preachers today who begin with a topic or a story. To Kinlaw, nothing is more important or more interesting than the Text. This is what makes his message so credible, even among his dissenters, and so relevant to every age. It is an important lesson for younger preachers today who are always tempted to pursue relevance, at the expense of the Text, and because of this to end up irrelevant.

In his book *The Mind of Christ*, he describes the holy life as one that is focused outward, instead of inward toward ourselves. "Outwardness is all there is to the gospel." Here is vintage Kinlaw, using Luther's phrase—*cor incurvitas ad se* ("man is curved inward upon himself")—to argue toward a Wesleyan doctrine of sanctification. In much of evangelical theology, sin is portrayed as an infraction against the Law, insofar as the Law expresses the perfect will of God. It is "any want of conformity to the will of God." In holiness theology we acknowledge this reality but emphasize even more that sin is a hindrance to the relationship—both actual and potential—between oneself and God. In holiness theology, the core of sin is not rebellion against a Sovereign (as in the Reformed tradition) but alienation from the Father, self-absorption and the loss of our full potential. Sanctification, then, is not merely being pious or sinless. It is a turning from inward to outward; from loving ourselves to loving God and serving others.

Kinlaw continually draws our eyes toward the source of spiritual vitality. By keeping the subject of holiness centered around the Person of Christ rather than the concept of "perfection," he has shown that God is more interested in giving us His nature than in giving us His will. Is it possible to be formed into the likeness of Christ? Is it realistic to continue in the belief that we can be given the mind of Christ? Kinlaw answers with an emphatic 'Yes!' with both his writing and his life.

—STEVE DENEFF

THE MIND OF CHRIST

Philippians 2:5–11 is the best-known passage of Scripture concerning the mind of Christ. Some modern translations render it in such a way that the word *mind* is not used; but Paul employs the same Greek verb that occurs in Mark 8, where Jesus tells Peter he does not think as God thinks. The Greek word (*phronite*) literally means, "to be minded"— in this case, to be minded as God is minded:

"Let each of you look not to your own interest, but to the interests of others. Let the same mind be in you that was in Christ Jesus, who, though he was in the form of God, did not regard equality with God as something to be exploited, but emptied himself, taking the form of a slave, being born in human likeness" (vv. 5–7).

Most scholars deal with verses 5–11 as if they were a unit, an ancient Christian hymn to the Christ. Perhaps they were. But I believe Paul used these words to illustrate the message he wished to convey to the Philippians.

A state of conflict existed within the Philippian church, and Paul wrote out of his desire to see that conflict resolved. Any time people work together, tension will develop. But unresolved tension brings reproach on the cause of Christ. Paul knew that this conflict could be resolved only if the Philippians had a change of heart—and a change of mind.

In chapter 1, Paul observes that some people preach Christ out of right motives, while others preach Christ out of contentiousness: 177 "Some proclaim Christ from envy and rivalry, but others from goodwill. These proclaim Christ out of love, knowing that I have been put there for the defense of the gospel; the others proclaim Christ out of selfish ambition..." (1:15–17a). Here Paul uses the Greek word *eritheia*, which literally means, "to strive." Paul condemns the tendency to contend for one's own way, which is at the heart of carnal thinking.

He introduces the second chapter with these words: "If then there is any encouragement in Christ, any consolation from love, any sharing in the Spirit, and compassion and sympathy, make my joy complete: be of the same mind, having the same love, being in full accord and of one mind" (2:1–2). The basic problem at Philippi was that the Christians had different "minds"; each one thought his own way. So if Paul was to heal their division, he had to deal with the mind. He describes the sort of mind they must have:

"Do nothing from selfish ambition [Gk., *eritheia*] or conceit, but in humility regard others as better than yourselves. Let each of you look not to your own interest, but the interest of others" (2:3–4).

The first time I read that in the Greek, I thought, *Wait a minute. Where is the word "only"?* The King James Version puts the word *only* in italics, which indicates it is not in the original Greek text. Try as I might, I couldn't find it in the Greek. So I went to our classical Greek specialist at the college, who has a Ph.D. in classical languages from St. Louis University, and I said, "Help me here." He cast about for a while and then wrote me a note that said: "It isn't there, Kinlaw."

I went to Bob Mulholland, who has a Ph.D. from Harvard in New Testament. I said, "Bob, I've got a question...." He pulled books down and looked all around his office. Finally, he said, "Kinlaw, it isn't there."

Now why is the word *only* inserted in that verse, in most modern translations of the Bible? Why do most versions read, "Let each of you look not *only* to your own interest, but also to the interest of others"? Because we twentieth-century Christians don't believe the Lord can deliver us from self-interest, so we insert our assumptions into Scripture.

FOUR UNGODLY CHARACTERISTICS

In verses 3 and 14, Paul lists four characteristics that should be alien to the Christian life. He says that every Christian should act (1) without self-interest: (2) with out vain conceit; (3) without grumbling; and (4) without questioning.

Self-interest (v. 3) is the supreme characteristic of a sinful person. It has been said that sinfulness is to be "curved inward upon one-self." Conversely, the purpose of the redemption offered by Christ is to undo our distorted orientation—to turn us outward, so that we are not interested in ourselves but in the well-being of others. When we understand sin in these terms, we begin to break down the traditional dichotomy between evangelism and Christian social action. After all, the Christian life is not an "either/or" proposition: "Either I enrich my own relationship with Christ, or I go out and show others who Christ is, through my selfless service." Outwardness is all there is to the gospel. The essence of Christian living is making oneself a servant, as Christ is a servant.

It is no accident that John Wesley became a paragon of Christian social action. He engaged in prison reform, slave emancipation, hospital work, and other activities that modern evangelicals sometimes disparage as the concerns of "the social gospel" (as if it were different

179

from the gospel of Christ). These activities were a normal consequence of Wesley's message about the necessity of entering into the Christ-life.

Self-interest is well demonstrated by the question, "What's in it for me?" Jesus never strived to get something for himself. The Gospels relate no instance in which Jesus' self-interest was his first consideration.

Imagine the scene when Jairus asked Jesus to heal his daughter. Suppose Jesus had said, "Yes, I could do that. I could go home with you and lay my hands on your daughter, and she would get well. *But what's in it for me?*" My mentioning such an idea must offend you, because that attitude is utterly antithetical to what Jesus represented. He came to lay down his life for his sheep (John 10:15). He did not come to protect himself; rather, he came to spend himself.

The Old Testament lifestyle may have been expressed by the statement, "Love your neighbor as yourself" (Lev. 19:18). But Jesus expressed the New Testament lifestyle like this: "Love one another as I have loved you. No one has greater love than this, to lay down one's life for one's friends" (John 15:12–13). Jesus changed the pattern of personal priorities when he became the Shepherd who sacrificed himself for his sheep.

HOW CAN WE HAVE THE MIND OF CHRIST

Becoming like Christ is a work of grace. It occurs only as Christ lives within us, not as we strive to be like him. Is this possible? Of course it is! Christian history is brimming with examples of men and women who have responded to life as Christ responded. They did it because Christ lived within them.

During Samuel Brengle's senior year at Boston University, he was offered the pastorate of a wealthy congregation in South Bend, Indiana. He had an opportunity to begin his ministry at the top of the social roster. But he felt that God was calling him to join the Salvation Army, so he crossed the Atlantic and presented himself to General William Booth.

"We don't want you. You're dangerous," Booth said.

"Dangerous? What do you mean?" Brengle asked.

"You would not take orders."

"But you haven't given me a trial," Brengle pleaded.

"You have too much education. You would not be willing to subordinate yourself to one of the officers here. Converted drunks and prostitutes are the staff leaders."

"Please give me a chance," Brengle said. So General Booth sent him to one of his sons, Ballington Booth, who put him through a similar interrogation. When Brengle still insisted on trying the Army, Booth's son made him bootblack for the Central Salvation Army Corps in London. In an unfinished basement, on a dirt floor half-submerged in water, Brengle began cleaning mud off of the boots of converted street bums who were now soldiers in the Army. One day he seemed to hear a voice that said, "You're a fool!"

I am not! he thought.

"You're a sinner, too."

What do you mean?

"Remember the man who buried his talent in the earth?" the inner voice said. "What are you doing here? Think of all the training you've gotten. You're just throwing it away." 181

DENNIS F. KINLAW

Brengle sank into a depression. After a while he prayed, "Lord, have I failed you? Did I miss your leading?"

And the Lord replied, "Remember, Sam, I washed their feet!"

That muddy cellar became an anteroom to heaven, as Brengle sensed the reassuring presence of his Lord. From that day forward, Brengle knew that he was called, not to invest himself, but to spend himself for others. He realized that Christ is a servant who looks for others to serve with him.

The Holy Spirit makes this sacrificial thinking possible. Jesus' ministry began when the Holy Spirit descended upon him. His disciples' ministry began when the Holy Spirit came upon them at the day of Pentecost, empowering them to "turn the world upside down." Likewise, the Spirit of Christ must control us if we are to be conformed to the character of Christ and filled with his power.

Christ must be free to spend us. As long as we attempt to save our own lives, we shall lose them; but if we surrender our lives to be controlled by his Spirit, we shall live and bear fruit for him. The Bible says very little about self-enrichment; but it says a great deal about giving our live for the enrichment of others.

This chapter is from Dennis F. Kinlaw's The Mind of Christ *and is used with the permission of Francis Asbury Press Box 7, Wilmore, KY 40390.*

KEITH **DRURY**

CHAPTER 20

YOU CAN DO IT.
YOU CAN BE CHRISTLIKE,
YOU CAN BE HOLY,
YOU CAN LIVE ABOVE SIN ...
WITH GOD'S HELP.

INTRODUCTION

The offer of a compelling "translation of holiness" is what has made this book so significant. *Holiness for Ordinary People* was written by Keith Drury (1945–), a denominational leader in the Wesleyan Church and later a professor at Indiana Wesleyan University. The book challenged us with the truths of biblical holiness, while offering uncomplicated hooks to hang those truths upon. If we had a somewhat fuzzy sense of what holiness was all about, *Holiness for Ordinary People* offered clarity. When some of us were tempted to water it down or throw it out, *Holiness for Ordinary People* offered the classic message explained in simple and accessible terms. The book offered a consistent opportunity for ordinary Christians to take an honest look at Scripture and their own experience, and find God could do something special and lasting to make them Christlike.

When this book emerged in the 1980s, trends didn't necessarily point toward a desire to hear more on the holiness message. After years of what Drury called the "sidetracks" or "tangents" from holiness—legalism, emotionalism, and so forth—the church was wondering what in fact to do with the "doctrine of holiness." While a translation of the doctrine was needed, *Holiness for Ordinary People* warned us not to throw the baby out with the bathwater.

The book itself was marked by the methods it employed. Extensive use of stories, dialogue, parables, and illustrations allowed the reader to enjoy the journey of learning about the *heart* of holiness. Drury's use of concise definitions, straightforward logic, concept summaries, practical examples, and even an FAQ-style opening chapter, the book became accessible to everyone—*ordinary* people. At the same time the book drew on the great *history* of holiness thinking throughout the ages and included direct testimonies of sanctification experience from a dozen leaders of the church, such as Dwight Moody, Catherine Booth, Charles Finney, Phoebe Palmer, and Billy Graham.

Drury not only explained holiness, he also emphasized the need for a thriving holiness *movement* to carry the *message*. In his address to the Christian Holiness Association in 1995, titled "The Holiness Movement Is Dead," he warned that we must not simply celebrate the *doctrine* of holiness but must also join the *new movement* of holiness when and where we see it emerging. That is our continued task for today.

Holiness for Ordinary People became just what its author wanted it to be: a translation of holiness for a generation. The lasting challenge of the book itself might be twofold. First, the book gave us a timeless and compelling draw to the simple but all-sanctifying way of Jesus Christ. Second, the book continues to challenge us to always be about the task of translation, so that every generation can know his call to the holy; that holiness might *spread across the land.*

—DAVID DRURY

THE WAY FORWARD

HOLINESS FOR ORDINARY PEOPLE

DEFINING HOLINESS AND SANCTIFICATION

Holiness is loving God with all my heart, mind, soul and strength, and loving my neighbor as myself. Simply put, holiness is Christlikeness. Holiness is not an "it" as in *"have you got it?"* It is *Him* I need. In Him I find purity, power, and obedience. Jesus Christ himself is the definition of holiness. As long as Jesus Christ is the central thrust of holiness teaching, He will keep us from flying off on a tangent. Anything more than Jesus is extra. He loved His Father and His neighbor perfectly—and thus was able to obey the Father perfectly. Love and obedience—one springs from the other. Holiness is *perfect love.*

Holiness is for every believer. Holiness isn't reserved for a select few of God's "teacher's pets," or just those people who live far above the ordinary humdrum of daily life. Holiness is not just for preachers, missionaries, and retired folk who "have enough time to pray all day." Holiness is for all of us. You really can love God with all of your heart, soul, mind, being, and strength. You actually can love your neighbor as you love yourself. You really can walk in obedience to God's known commands. You are not stuck with an endless cycle of defeat in your Christian life. Holiness is possible in this life! Understanding doctrine is important. But experiencing God's grace is even more important.

Sanctification is everything God does in us to make us more Christlike. *Everything.* Our sanctification begins at conversion, progresses as we grow in grace, leads us to the point of entire sanctification, and then continues beyond that point—until the day we die, 187 perhaps even beyond. Sanctification is God's Spirit at work in our mind, soul, spirit, body—our entire life—changing and renewing our desires, thoughts, interests, attitudes, and behaviors. Sanctification is how God transforms us into His Son's likeness. Such a believer will eventually become increasingly active in caring for the rejected, widowed, orphaned, poor, jailed, or others in distress and need. Soon this Christian will actually start searching for opportunities to use personal resources to aid others.

THE PROCESS OF SANCTIFICATION

God wants total and complete commitment. Complete obedience. Jesus reinforced this high standard of holiness. He established it as the "most important commandment." We are commanded to love God with all our heart, soul, mind, and strength—our whole being—not with part and not even with most of our being. All means just that: all. 100 percent. No less.

Then, just in case we are tempted to become holy recluses, Jesus attaches the second command: "Love your neighbor as yourself." These two commands—loving God and loving our neighbor—provide the clear standard of holiness. Jesus summarized here the holiness teaching found throughout the Bible. God is holy. He expects us to be holy. Holiness is loving devotion to God and others. We can live this way only through His power.

The term *sanctification* refers to everything God does in us to make us more like Christ. It is a global word. It includes the following:

188

- *Initial Sanctification*—what God does at conversion to change and transform us.

- *Progressive sanctification*—God's gradual work which helps us gradually grow in grace as believers.

- *Entire sanctification or "Baptism with the Holy Spirit"*—God's work of cleansing and empowering following our total consecration to Him.

- *Continual sanctification*—God's continual daily cleansing of us as Spirit-baptized believers, making us more Christlike in every word, thought, deed, and attitude.

- *Final sanctification: "Glorification"*—God's final transformation of us at death, completing His work and preparing us for heaven.

All five of these aspects or stages of sanctification are biblical. Sometimes people confuse one stage with another. The terms may seem confusing, but don't let them scare you away.

QUESTIONS TO ASK YOURSELF

Does my heart well up with love for other people: those who are unfriendly or unkind; the poor, helpless, and needy; those without Jesus Christ; even those who consider themselves my enemies? Is there any remaining bitterness, envy, jealousy, unforgiving spirit, or wrath toward any other man or woman? Do I entirely love others as much as I love and care for myself? These are evidences of perfect love for others, which God creates in us.

Can you say that there is no willful disobedience in your life right now? Is there something God has clearly convicted you is wrong, yet you continue to do it? Or say it? Or think it? Is there anything God is specifically directing you to do, yet you are refusing to do it? Are you 189 deciding to disobey the Lord in any area of your life?

Has God changed your orientation toward others so that your heart and will are completely committed to love them? Are you becoming perfect in love as Christ is?

Do *you* have an undivided heart? Can you say that your heart is totally magnetized toward Christ? Are you fully committed to obedience? Is Christ's will the central focus of your life? What do you want most out of life? Is it obedience to His will? Is obedience to Christ the consuming passion of your heart?

REFLECTIONS ON THE RECEPTION OF THE BOOK

Perhaps the continued usefulness of this book *[Holiness for Ordinary People]* tells us more about the subject than about the author—and that we are in need of men and women to be living examples of what it means to be a "fully devoted follower of Jesus Christ." Since the book's release, I have been delighted most of all by the reception of this book by the young. Newer generations are not burdened by the baggage of past errors and excesses associated with this biblical doctrine. They come to the Bible and take it at face value. Since God calls us to love Him with all of our heart, soul, mind, and strength, they presume one can actually obey this command. And they hunger to know how. This interest among the young is perhaps the greatest reason to be optimistic about the future of the church.

THE CHALLENGE OF HOLY LIVING

Confusion about the sanctified life is common. Some have even painted such an absurd picture of what it means to be sanctified completely that it has chased people away from seeking the experience. Others have the notion that this walk with God transforms people into

190

spiritual giants, raising them above all human weakness and temptation. They even expect a life of constant emotional exultation and joy. This is simply not true.

Holiness is not a doctrine designed to bludgeon honest believers into despair by telling them they are defective. It is a message of hope, encouragement, and possibility. It marches into your life, saying, "You can do it. You can be Christlike, you can be holy, you can live above sin . . . with God's help. The one who calls you is faithful . . . He will do it."

Don't respond in despair or in doubt. If you are sincerely interested in the whole matter of becoming fully Christlike, keep seeking! If you are not totally convinced that living obediently is possible, keep searching. Don't become closed-minded on the subject.

This truth is for ordinary people. It is for you. Hunger and you will be filled. Seek and you will find!

KEITH DRURY